ALL KINDS OF MINDS

ALL KINDS OF MINDS

A Young Student's Book about Learning Abilities and Learning Disorders

Dr. Mel Levine

Educators Publishing Service, Inc.
Cambridge and Toronto

Illustrations by Daisy de Puthod
Cover design by Hugh Price
Text design by Joyce C. Weston

Printed in U.S.A.

ISBN 0-8388-2090-5

Educators Publishing Service, Inc., 31 Smith Place,
Cambridge, MA 02138-1000

December, 1995 Printing

This book is dedicated to all of those caring teachers who are kind to every kind of mind.

Contents

1. All Kinds of Minds

The First Day of School

On the first day of school, a big yellow school bus arrived at the corner right on time. A young girl climbed inside and began to talk very fast.

"Don't leave! Please wait!" she said. "Eddie's on his way. He had trouble getting out of bed. Then it took him too long to get dressed. That's 'cause he couldn't find one of his shoes. That's 'cause he put the shoe in his backpack. He really meant to put his reading book in it. I found his backpack under the bathroom sink. He must have left it there when he brushed his teeth. I don't know why he needed his backpack to brush his teeth!"

The bus driver looked annoyed. "Becky," he said, "I heard these same stories all last year. Let's not go through them again. If your brother doesn't get here in one minute, I'm leaving without him. And this is the last time I'll wait for him at all. You tell him that."

Moments later, Eddie came running down the sidewalk. Even though it was raining, he was carrying his baseball cap and his raincoat, which was dragging behind him in the mud. His shoelaces were untied, and his backpack was on top of his head. But there were no books in the backpack. Only a big red skateboard was sticking out. A little white dog with a big brown spot on his back chased after Eddie.

"Sorry! Sorry!" Eddie shouted as he jumped

onto the bus. "I didn't mean to be late. How about if we guys all attach our skateboards to the bus to make it go faster? Then, we won't be late for school. Wouldn't that be cool?"

The bus driver looked at Eddie sternly and said, "You'd better settle down, or I might have to report you again. And just remember: this is the last time I'll wait for you. I told you last year I wasn't going to put up with this late stuff anymore."

Eddie sat down and started talking to the kid next to him. He was talking very loud, and the bus driver turned around and stared at him.

After that, Eddie got quiet. "Here I go again," he thought to himself. "More trouble. I never *mean* to get into trouble. Why do I always have to get into trouble?"

As the bus pulled away, two big dogs appeared and started to chase Eddie's little white dog with the brown back. Fortunately, Eddie's dog managed to escape from the dog bullies.

The bus continued down the road. A few blocks later, it stopped again. Two girls got on and sat next to each other. One was Sonya. She was very quiet as she looked out the window. The other girl, Eve, seemed a little scared. She stared at the floor. She looked as if she had been crying.

At the next stop, a small group of children got on. One of them was a tall, strong boy carrying a soccer ball. He sat down and started to toss the ball up into the air and catch it again. The bus driver made him stop that. Then the boy began to spin the ball on his finger. He seemed to be trying to get into trouble with the driver. But really he was playing with the ball so he wouldn't have to think about school. He hated to think about school. He looked angry.

In a little while, the bus arrived at the last stop before the school. A boy with two book bags full of books started to climb into the bus. As he put one foot on the first step, he fell back to the ground. Some books in one bag fell out into the mud. Several kids laughed. The boy picked up his books and tried to wipe them off with his jacket. Then, he got on the bus, went to the back, and sat down by himself.

Someone said, "Hey, Derek, how come you have all those books?"

"These are just *some* of the many books I read this summer," the boy answered. "I'm taking them to show the teacher. She'll be amazed at how many books I read and how hard they are."

Bill, the boy with the soccer ball, looked up. "Nobody cares how many nerdy books you read or how hard they are," he snapped.

Derek answered, "You're just jealous. That's all. You wish you could read hard books like me." Bill jumped up, looking as if he were going to grab Derek.

The driver turned around and made everyone sit down.

Finally, the bus arrived at school. Eddie made rocket noises as he zoomed toward the building.

Eve and Sonya, looking worried, walked slowly. Bill dribbled his soccer ball up the stairs and into the hall. And Derek nearly bumped into a tree as he tried to read and walk at the same time.

Everyone headed toward their classroom and their new teacher, Mrs. Grillo. These kids, like most kids, wanted to be smart in school and popular and good at sports. But each kid was afraid that school would be tough or embarrassing again this year.

What *All Kinds of Minds* Is About

All Kinds of Minds will show us that different children have different kinds of minds.

As we shall see, the children we met on the bus are the stars of this book. All of them are really "neat" kids. But each one has some problems with his or her kind of mind. That's not unusual, though. All kids have some problems. No one's life is perfect. And no one's mind is perfect.

In this book, we will learn a whole lot more about the children on the bus. We will see that these kids were worried or angry because they knew their minds weren't working well enough in school.

Many kids go to school feeling bad about themselves. They feel bad because their minds have a hard time with certain kinds of mind work in school. Actually, there's no such thing as a mind that does every kind of mind work well. Different minds are good at different kinds of mind work. And, as your mind gets better and better at different kinds of mind work, the mind *work* gets to be mind *fun!*

Weaknesses in a student's mind can make it very hard to do certain kinds of mind work. These weaknesses are often called **learning disorders**. Sometimes they are called **learning disabilities**. We will learn a lot about learning disorders and about kids like the children on the bus, students who have learning disorders.

Learning disorders can make kids very sad so they worry a lot. Often, kids don't really understand their learning disorders. They really don't know much about their own kinds of minds. They may not have thought about all the different kinds of mind work they have to do in school every day. You can see a description of some of the different kinds of mind work on page 10.

After you have read *All Kinds of Minds* or listened to the tapes, you should understand learning disorders much better. You will probably get some good ideas about how to work on any learning disorders that your kind of mind might have. And, remember, nobody has a perfect mind!

Some Kinds of Mind Work

Your mind is the thinking part of your brain. Your mind always has a lot of work to do. Here are some kinds of mind work that your mind needs to do.

Concentrating
When you concentrate, you pay attention. This means you think about or look at or listen to the right thing at the right time. It also means that you pay attention long enough.

Building Up Skills
You use your mind in school to build up skills like reading, writing, spelling, and doing arithmetic.

Remembering
Your mind is like a dresser or a desk with a lot of drawers in it. It stores things. This means it remembers what you need to know—like spelling words, vocabulary, or the names of your friends.

Getting Things in the Right Order
Your mind works at understanding and remembering things in the right order—like knowing your telephone number or the alphabet. Getting things in the right order is called sequencing.

Understanding Things That You See
Your mind understands how things look and how they go together. It tells you what's big and what's small, what's round and what's square, what's on top and what's on bottom.

Understanding and Using Words and Sentences
Your mind helps you understand language. It also figures out how you can say or write your ideas.

Making Muscles Work	Your mind gets your muscles to work smoothly and quickly. This way, you can do things like write, tie your shoelaces, and play sports.
Having Ideas and Solving Problems	Your mind thinks up good ideas and helps you know what to do when you have to solve a problem (like a problem in arithmetic or a problem you're having with your bicycle).
Helping to Make and Keep Friends	Your mind helps you figure out how to get other kids to like you.

The Rest of This Book

In *All Kinds of Minds*, there is a chapter about each of the kids we met on the bus. Each of these chapters tells you a lot about one kid's kind of mind. You will learn about the kinds of mind work that are easy and the kinds of mind work that are hard for each student. In other words, you will find out about each kid's strengths and about any learning disorders that he or she has. Chapter 7 is about all of these children and what they might be like when they grow up.

Chapter 8, the last chapter in the book, reviews some important ideas about different kinds of learning disorders and the minds that have these disorders. It also describes some things that can be done to help students who have these problems.

When you have finished *All Kinds of Minds*, you will realize how cruel it is to make fun of other children because of the ways their minds work. You will also see that you should never feel too bad about the way your own kind of mind works. So, this book will help you be kind to all kinds of minds.

2. Eddie's Kind of Mind

Other kids liked Eddie a whole lot. They thought he was fun, and they thought he was funny. Eddie loved excitement. He was always ready for a good time. That's why his friends liked to call him Ever-Ready-Eddie.

Eddie had some awesome ideas. He loved to invent far-out things. He never actually made these things. He just liked to think them up. And he loved to talk about them.

One day he told everyone he was going to

make a remote-control teacher-tickler-zapper. He said he'd keep it on his desk in school. When he pressed a button on his teacher-tickler-zapper, his teacher would start laughing and laughing. She wouldn't be able to stop laughing until he pushed another button on the zapper.

Eddie thought this invention would be excellent whenever he got into trouble in class. As soon as the teacher started to correct him, he could point his super invention at her and press a button. Then she would have to start laughing.

Eddie loved animals. He and his twin sister Becky had a dog named Hot Fudge. Hot Fudge was white with a big brown spot on his back that looked like chocolate. He loved Eddie and Becky, and they loved him. But other dogs seemed to hate Hot Fudge. They didn't think Hot Fudge was so hot. They often tried to attack him and make him cry.

Eddie thought about inventing a computer to use with dogs. He'd call it a bark processor

because it would help him understand dog talk. When Hot Fudge barked or growled, it would turn his barks into English words. That way Eddie would be able to understand what his dog was telling him. Eddie also wanted to be able to change *his* words into barks. Then Hot Fudge could understand Eddie better, too.

Hot Fudge was very smart, and Eddie knew it. That dog never forgot anything. He could remember where he had left his toys. And he always knew what time Eddie and Becky would be getting home from school. He'd be right there at the bus stop.

Eddie had a good memory, too—at least for some things. He could remember little things from long ago without any trouble. One time, when he was very young, he and Becky went on a long car trip with their parents. Five years later, Eddie could still remember everything about the trip.

He could remember what they had eaten for lunch when they finally reached his grandparents' house. He could even describe the gas stations they had passed along the way.

Eddie's Attention in School

Mrs. Grillo, Eddie's teacher, kept saying Eddie had a terrific mind. Still, he couldn't seem to get his work done. He looked as if he wasn't really trying to get it done.

In the classroom, Eddie often had trouble sitting still. His arms and legs kept wanting to move. He would tap his feet and his pencil. He would get out of his seat. Sometimes he would ask to go to the boys' room just to keep moving.

When Eddie did sit at his desk, his body often looked all twisted up. You'd think he was trying to tie his legs in knots. He liked to sit on one of his feet. He would put one arm behind his head and his other arm under his chin. At times like this, Eddie looked like a living pretzel!

Sometimes Eddie's teacher, Mrs. Grillo, got

upset because Eddie didn't listen to what he was supposed to. He might *start* to listen to the teacher. But then his mind would switch to something else.

When Mrs. Grillo was explaining something to the class, Eddie would often stare out the window. He might think about the far-off future. He might think about what he was going to do after school. Sometimes he would listen to noises outside—like an airplane flying overhead. Or he would daydream.

A lot of the time, Eddie wouldn't hear anything Mrs. Grillo was saying. Eddie once told Mrs. Grillo that he had trouble listening because his mind "took trips." Eddie said, "My mind takes long trips—like into outer space."

One day, Mrs. Grillo was teaching a science lesson about frogs. Sonya, a girl in Eddie's class, had brought in a jar full of tadpoles. Mrs. Grillo was explaining that female frogs lay eggs. She said that the eggs change into tadpoles, and the tadpoles grow up to be frogs.

Eddie looked at the tadpoles in the jar. Then his mind took off. He decided that the tadpoles looked like little submarines. He began to imagine riding in a super submarine. It would have legs that could come out like a tadpole's when it was turning into a frog.

This frog-legged submarine could leap out of water onto land. It could also pull in its legs and

grow wings and fly up over buildings to the tops of mountains. Its engines could even make it soar into outer space.

When it needed to go back under water, it could pull in its wings quickly. "Cool! Excellent!" Eddie thought to himself. He was right in the middle of a flying frog-legged submarine dive.

Suddenly, just when Eddie was pulling in the wings to plunge under the ocean, Mrs. Grillo called on him. "Eddie?" she said. "How many eggs can a frog lay?"

Eddie didn't even hear the question!

Mrs. Grillo repeated it. This time Eddie heard the question, but he couldn't answer it.

Mrs. Grillo had been telling the class about frog eggs. But Eddie's mind had been somewhere between the Pacific Ocean and Mars on his flying frog-legged submarine.

That's what kept happening to Eddie. He'd go off on exciting mind trips and miss important ideas in class.

Eddie never had trouble paying attention when he was doing something he enjoyed a lot—like playing a video game. But school work or chores at home made Eddie's mind stop paying attention.

One day Eddie was watching television. He got the idea that his mind was just like a broken television set that kept changing channels all by itself. He got to see many programs. But as soon as he started to watch one program, another one would come onto his mind's screen. He could never finish a program.

Eddie's School Work

Eddie seemed so smart. He could read well. But a lot of his other school work was terrible. He hated to write. Writing was a kind of mind work that was always tough for Eddie. His writing was messy and hard to read. He couldn't get it to look right. Eddie said writing was boring. It took too long. He liked to think fast and do things quickly.

Eddie hated to stop and plan and think about what to say and how to say it. And Eddie couldn't stand to check his work for things like spelling errors, so he made a lot of mistakes. Writing was the hardest thing in school for him.

Eddie was pretty good at arithmetic. He understood how numbers worked. He could remember arithmetic facts very easily. For example, he could quickly tell you how much 7×8 is. But often Eddie would not get the correct answers when he did problems. That seemed strange to everyone.

How could Eddie understand arithmetic so well and yet fail a lot of arithmetic tests? It was because Eddie's mind ran much too fast. So he made lots of careless mistakes. His mind wouldn't notice whether there was a plus sign or a minus sign in a problem. He would see a 3 and think it was a 2 because he looked at the number too fast.

Eddie also hated to look back over his math problems to check for mistakes. To him, that was boring. It took too long. He always felt so glad to be done with his work.

Remembering important things in school was not so easy for Eddie, either. Sometimes, at the end of the day, he couldn't even remember what books to take home.

Eddie at Home

Eddie's mother and father thought that Eddie was fun to be with. He said and did so many neat things. They also loved his exciting ideas and his fantastic inventions.

However, Eddie's parents sometimes got very angry at him. This was mainly because he didn't listen. His mother had to say things three, four, or five times to get him to obey her. When she

told Eddie to clean up his room, he didn't seem to hear a word! His room looked like a total garbage dump. He never put anything away. There were huge piles of stuff everywhere.

Eddie's parents said that when Eddie wanted something, he wanted it too much. He kept asking and asking and asking for it. He couldn't seem to wait. When he went into a store, he always seemed to want something very badly. He got upset if he couldn't have it right away.

And Eddie wanted so many things and so much action. He constantly wanted to do things, go places, and get things. Often when he got what he wanted, Eddie wanted something else, too. Eddie's parents said he was really hard to satisfy.

Falling asleep at night was often a problem for Eddie. That was because his mind was very active, even when he was trying to go to sleep.

When Eddie finally got to sleep, his body stayed active. He kicked the covers off his bed. Sometimes he pushed his pillow onto the floor.

When Hot Fudge was a puppy, he used to sleep on Eddie's bed. But he stopped doing that because Eddie moved around too much.

Eddie had a hard time waking up in the morning, too. It was torture for him to get out of bed and get dressed. It always seemed as if his clothes weighed a ton. Sometimes, his father had to drag Eddie out of the bed. When it came to getting ready for school or for anything except fun, he was Never-Ready-Eddie. Eddie's sister Becky was always ready for school long before Eddie.

Eddie and Becky argued a lot. Becky did very well in school. Her room was always neat. The twins' parents had no trouble with Becky.

Eddie liked to bother Becky. He liked to stir things up when she was around. He called her "Ecky-Becky," and she called him a yucky brat.

Almost every day, Eddie did something to make his sister angry. Sometimes he unplugged the telephone while she was talking. Once he put a worm in her bed. He hid her sneakers in the refrigerator and put pepper in her cereal. Still, Eddie and Becky kind of liked to do things together.

Lunch at the Mall

One Saturday, Eddie, Becky, and their friend Sonya went to the mall with their mothers. Eddie called it The Spend-It-All Shopping Mall. He wanted to take his skateboard, but his mother wouldn't let him. She said that skateboarding was not allowed in the mall. Eddie also wanted to take Hot Fudge. But dogs weren't allowed inside the mall, either.

The two mothers decided that the children should have lunch by themselves while the grown-ups did an errand. They took Eddie, Becky, and Sonya to a part of the mall where there were places to eat, and they gave each child some money to buy lunch. The mothers said that they would be back in about twenty minutes.

Just before she left to go shopping, Eddie's mother said to him, "Eddie, I want you to behave yourself. Don't do anything silly. Don't bother other people. Don't fight with your sister. And don't play with your food. Just behave and eat your lunch."

Eddie answered, "Mom, have no fear. Ever-Ready-Eddie will be a super-excellent-perfect-great kid. People will say that you are the mother of the world's best-behaved, model child. Everyone in town will want their kids to have lunch with Eddie, the boy with the perfect manners, the most wonderful behavior, the coolest looks, and the creepiest sister in the world!"

Eddie's mother answered, "Just behave, Eddie, or I'll never be able to leave you alone with other kids like this."

The two mothers left, and the children looked at the list of food on the wall at one of the places to eat. It was called *Big Frank's Big Franks.* Behind the counter stood a very big man cooking food on a grill.

Eddie said, "I know what I want. I'd like a ten-foot-long frankfurter with everything on it and five gallons of soda, ten pounds of french fries, two bottles of catsup, and a strawberry and coffee ripple ice cream sundae with hot fudge, cold butterscotch, bananas, coconut, peanut butter, and chopped peppermint Life Savers. Oh, and I'd also like a side order of mustard custard."

Eddie's sister laughed, but she looked annoyed. "That sounds real yucky," she said. "Besides, you don't have enough money to pay for all that."

Eddie said, "Oops! I forgot. I guess I'll just have a good old hot dog and a coke."

Becky asked, "What are you having, Sonya?"

Sonya answered, "I think I'll have two slices of pizza."

Eddie roared with laughter. "Pizza?" he shouted. "Pizza? There's no pizza on the menu on the wall! They only have hamburgers and hot dogs and stuff like that.

"What's the matter, Sonya? Can't you read? Can't you read something simple like that sign? Boy, are you a dummy! You can't even tell the difference between the words *pizza* and *frank*. No wonder you get all that special headucation in school."

Sonya said quietly, "I'm not a dummy. I'm not stupid, you weirdo. I can read okay. I can read a little. Besides, it's special *education*, not *headucation!*"

Then Becky said, "Be quiet, Eddie. Let's just eat. I want a hot dog and french fries. What do you want, Sonya?"

Sonya answered, "I'll have the same thing."

Big Frank got the children their food. They found a table and sat down together.

Eddie Gets into Trouble

Almost as soon as Eddie sat down, he went off on one of his mind trips. On the table, there was a plastic mustard bottle. It reminded Eddie of a fire-breathing dragon, a solid gold fire-breathing dragon.

Eddie yelled to the girls, "Be careful! Be careful! You could get burned by fuming fang fire from the gold-fanged mustard monster! Beware of this dragon's gigantic, flaming fangs when he opens his fire mouth. At any moment, he may leap up into the sky and spray mustard fire all over everything and everybody."

Eddie grabbed a bowl with little bags of sugar in it. He folded a napkin and stuck it in the bowl. Next, he took two forks and put them into the bowl with the prong ends up. After that, he put the plastic mustard bottle into the sugar between the two forks.

Eddie said, "See the fork fangs and the napkin wings of the golden fighting-exciting-biting-igniting mustard dragon?

"Okay, everybody. Be careful. Beware. Be ready. The sizzling hot mustard dragon is about to fire his first fierce fire. Get set. Get your firefighter shields ready. Here goes the attack of the incredible gold-fanged mustard monster!"

Then, with all his might, Eddie squeezed the plastic mustard bottle. Mustard sprayed all over the place.

The girls jumped up in surprise. The golden mustard dragon tumbled out of the sugar bowl, which fell onto the floor and broke. As the girls jumped back, a salt shaker fell off the table, and it broke too. Then the catsup bottle turned over and spilled.

Sonya's tee shirt was splattered with mustard, and her arms were spotted with catsup. A big glob of mustard had landed on the tip of Becky's nose. Eddie's hands were splashed with a mixture of mustard and catsup, plus a sprinkling of sugar.

Big Frank came running over. He looked extremely angry. He said to Eddie, "Look what you've done! Just look at it! I don't know why your mother left you here. You can't be trusted. You'll have to pay for all this."

Sonya started to get up and said, "I'm going to find my mother."

Everyone at the other tables was looking at Eddie. They seemed to be talking about his behavior. Eddie felt so ashamed.

Eddie yelled, "No, don't! Don't! I'll clean up. I'll clean everything up. I'll sell my hot dog and use the money to pay for the damage. Don't tell Mom. She'll be so mad. I'll be in big, serious, terrible, awful, horrible trouble."

Eddie looked scared. He couldn't believe what he had done. Everything had happened so fast. He couldn't believe he had made such a huge mess.

Becky said, "Sonya, we have to stay here. Our moms told us not to leave until they come back."

All Sonya could say was, "Eddie is *so* bad!"

This made Eddie very angry. He said, "Don't tell our mothers. If you tell them what happened, I'll tell everyone at school you can't read. They'll think you're too stupid to read.

"And, Becky, if you tell Mom, I'll tell everybody at school you wet your bed. That's *your* biggest secret. And I'll tell it to everybody!"

Sonya was shocked. She said, "Becky, you wet your bed? Do you *really* wet your bed?"

Becky answered, "I don't feel like talking. Let's just stay here and eat."

Eddie Feels Sorry

Big Frank came over and started to clean off the table. Eddie picked up some pieces of broken glass. He said, "I'm sorry. I'm really, really sorry.

And I'm not bad. It all happened so fast. I did it so fast. I didn't mean to break those glasses. Please don't tell anyone—especially my mother! She'll never take me anywhere again." Eddie was beginning to cry.

Big Frank felt bad for Eddie. He saw that Eddie was really sorry. He said, "Okay, I'll forget about this. And I'll get it cleaned up before your mothers get back. But the next time you come in here, you'd better behave yourself. If you don't, you'll have to leave."

Eddie said, "Definitely. I'll be super good next time."

Eddie Worries

That night Eddie had a hard time falling asleep. He kept thinking about what had happened at the mall. He had not meant to get into trouble. He *never* meant to get into trouble. He just *got* into trouble. When he started to do something wrong, his mind didn't notice that he was getting into trouble.

When Eddie finally fell asleep, he dreamed that he was in a bus. It was going too fast, and it didn't have a driver to steer it or put the brakes on.

When he woke up, Eddie worried that maybe he was a mental case or just too dumb to act right. Eddie felt very sad and a little scared. He didn't know what kind of trouble he might get into next.

Eddie Learns about His Problem

Eddie's parents felt confused about their son. They loved him so much. They knew he was a great kid. He often was a lot of fun, and he had a super imagination. But his poor work in school and his behavior were big problems.

Eddie's parents decided to have a talk with Mrs. Grillo. She thought that Eddie should go to a doctor who helps kids with learning and behavior problems.

When Eddie first heard about this idea, he didn't like it. He didn't want to go to a doctor. He was afraid. He thought the doctor might operate on his brain. Eddie was also worried that the other kids might find out he was going to a "mental doctor."

Eddie's parents told him that lots of kids go to doctors for help with learning and behavior problems. They also told Eddie he would not have any kind of brain operation. They explained that it is important for everyone to understand his or her mind better. His father said that Eddie had to understand his mind better, too.

Eddie's parents took him to see Dr. Bronson, a **pediatrician**. Dr. Bronson had gotten some information from Eddie's teacher. He talked to Eddie and his parents for a long time. They discussed Eddie's school work and his behavior at home.

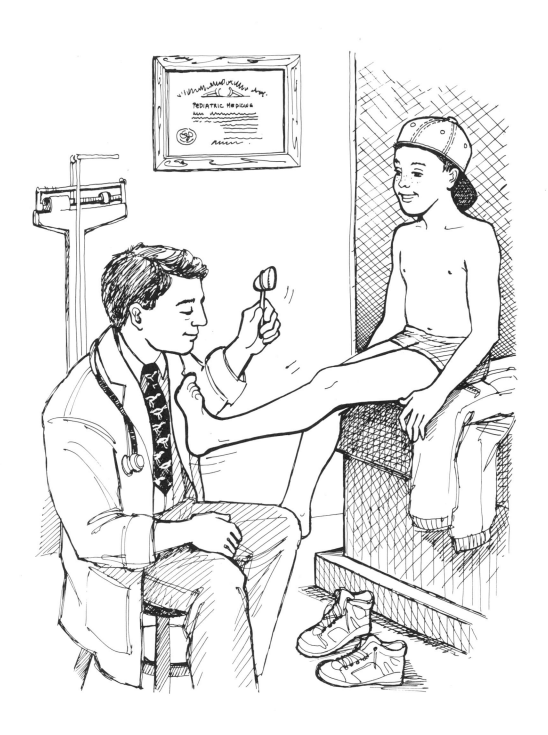

Dr. Bronson also gave Eddie a complete checkup. He did different things to make sure that Eddie's brain and nerves were working right. He checked Eddie's reflexes. He used a rubber hammer and tapped just below Eddie's knees. Eddie's reflexes were great. In fact, he just about kicked the doctor in the chin!

Dr. Bronson told Eddie that he was very healthy. He was strong and growing well. Then he gave Eddie some tests. These were like puzzles and games. They helped the doctor understand Eddie's way of learning and thinking.

After all the tests were done, Dr. Bronson met with Eddie and his parents. The doctor explained that Eddie was very smart but that he had a learning disorder called an **attention deficit**. This meant that he had trouble paying attention or concentrating. The doctor told the family that attention deficits are very common. They are sometimes called **ADD** or **ADHD**.

Dr. Bronson said, "It's hard for children with

attention deficits to do certain kinds of mind work. They have problems when they have to sit still and listen. Many of these kids like to move around a lot. When they try to sit and listen in school, their minds get tired, and they feel bored. They have trouble finishing something they start unless it's very exciting."

Eddie wondered, "How does he know? That happens to me all the time!"

Dr. Bronson continued, "Even when their bodies don't move a lot, most children with attention deficits have very active minds. They think about unimportant things. They pay attention to things that aren't really important at the time."

"Yeah," said Eddie. "That happens to me a lot. Like, sometimes in class while the teacher is talking, I start playing video games in my head."

Dr. Bronson nodded and said, "Often, when a teacher is explaining something, kids with attention deficits don't pay attention. Instead, they listen to a clock or stare at a fly on the window sill. Kids like this are called **distractible**. The little things they pay attention to are called **distractions**."

What the doctor said reminded Eddie of his mind trips.

Doctor Bronson said that most children with attention deficits are **impulsive**. That means they do a lot of things too quickly without thinking.

"Yup, that's me," Eddie thought to himself.

Dr. Bronson said that doing things too fast without thinking can cause behavior problems. (Eddie remembered how he had gotten into trouble at the mall.) Eddie learned that doing things too fast can cause problems in school, too. It can make a kid's work sloppy.

"An attention deficit is usually something you are born with," Dr. Bronson explained.

Eddie's father laughed. "I was a lot like Eddie when I was young," he said.

Eddie's father was now an architect. He

designed houses and tall buildings. He loved his work and could pay attention to it very well.

Dr. Bronson told Eddie that his learning problems and some of his behavior were not completely his fault. He said that often Eddie couldn't help it when he did things too fast or when he took a mind trip.

He also told Eddie that many, many people with attention deficits are very successful when they grow up. They have great ideas. They can do a lot of things in a short time. Hearing this made Eddie feel better.

He spoke up. "I'm really, really glad to hear there are other kids in the world like me," he said. "I thought I was the only one, the world's one and only totally weird kid!"

Dr. Bronson said that Eddie could make his attention get stronger.

- First, he would have to understand his attention deficit.
- Second, he would have to think hard about

his attention when he was in the classroom.

- Third, he would have to take more time to think *before* he did things. For example, he would have to think about what would happen before he played a trick on his sister. He would need to think about what would happen before he said something silly in class. In other words, Eddie needed to work on slowing down and thinking before doing things.

Dr. Bronson thought it would be a good idea for Eddie to take some pills to help his attention. "Pills don't always work," the doctor said. "But often they help kids concentrate better.

"Pills can help you slow down your mind so you can plan what you do. They help your mind stay 'tuned in' so you can think about and listen to the right things. In other words, they help you think harder in school."

Dr. Bronson said that pills could not

completely change Eddie. And Eddie could not take the pills all his life.

Eddie would also have to *work* on making his attention stronger.

"Eddie, there are many parts of you that no one wants to change at all," Dr. Bronson said. "Everyone hopes you'll keep thinking up great ideas and saying funny things. No one wants a whole new Eddie. We all just want to help you with the parts of your mind that are making life hard for you at school and at home."

Dr. Bronson also suggested that Eddie have a tutor to help him think harder, listen better, plan more, and check things over more carefully.

Eddie Gets Help

There are several kinds of attention pills. The ones Eddie took are called Ritalin. He wanted his dog Hot Fudge to take the pills, too. Eddie's mother said no. Hot Fudge's mind didn't take trips at the wrong times the way Eddie's did.

Eddie also began to see a **tutor**. She was a special teacher who helped him study and learn better. Her office was near Eddie's house. He went there once a week after school.

Eddie's parents talked to his sister Becky. They told her all about Eddie's attention deficit. The whole family now understood Eddie better. Dr. Bronson wrote a report about Eddie. Mrs. Grillo read it so she also could understand Eddie better and do things to help him.

Mrs. Grillo put a little card on Eddie's desk. It was there to help him concentrate. It reminded him not to take long mind trips when he needed to be listening. Whenever Eddie stopped a mind trip before it went very far, he put a check mark on the card. This helped him a lot.

Mrs. Grillo also told Eddie to keep a pencil in his hand while he was listening in class. She said he should try to write down a few of her words as she talked. This helped him pay attention, too.

Eddie sat up front, close to Mrs. Grillo. Every time she noticed that his mind was going off on a trip, she would touch his shoulder. The other kids didn't notice this. But Eddie could tell it meant he needed to tune in to the teacher again.

Mrs. Grillo knew that Eddie was very good at drawing. She helped him draw pictures of his inventions. He loved drawing cars, space vehicles, and, of course, flagship-frogships.

Eddie began to do a lot of swimming because it let him keep moving. Eddie loved moving around instead of staying still all the time. He joined a swim team and got better and better at swimming.

He also learned to play the drums. His parents made sure, though, that he had plenty of free time to use his imagination. That way he could still make up games and do a lot of pretending. Eddie's kind of mind loved to make believe.

Eddie started to feel better and better about being Eddie. He looked forward to a time when he could stop taking the pills. That would mean his mind could control his attention on its own. He knew this would happen one day.

Eddie no longer thought he was dumb or crazy or bad. He realized that every mind has some problems. His problems were with attention, and he was working on them. Eddie wrote a letter to his doctor. You can see what it said on page 49.

Dear. Docter bronson

At firs I was afrade to go and see you.

I was scard you would giv me shots or do a brain operatioun on me. I was afrade youd tell my parince that I was a sereyes mentel case or a totle severe domy,

In stead you told us about my atintion defenet Now that I know abote it I can do somthins about it I am working on it my atinthoun is a problem but it's not as bad as I thought and I'm not as bad as I thought I do bad things som times but I'm not a bad kid and now I know it's not wrong to have mind trips as long as your mind doasnt travel to fair aray at the rong times

I thinh my itinthoun will get stroner and strger and I will get to be even more ever read and super steady eddie

thanks
your pall
ever read
eddie

PS. I'm sorry my foot hit your chin wen you banged my nee

49

3. Sonya's Kind of Mind

Sonya was very good at doing things with her hands. When something was broken, she could often figure out what was wrong with it. Her father called her "Ms. Fix It." She was also very good at making things look nice. She loved to decorate everything.

One day Sonya's father bought a dog house for their puppy Chewsy who liked to chew on everything. Sonya's father said Chewsy was not very choosy about her chewing!

Sonya wanted to make their dog's house look really great. So she got out her paints and went to work. On the back, she painted a bone that looked good enough to chew. On the sides, she painted windows. She even nailed cloth on them to look like curtains. Sonya spent hours working on the dog house. She loved to make things look excellent. Chewsy seemed pleased, too. But she couldn't figure out why the bone on the back of her house didn't smell like a bone. And she wondered why she couldn't get it off!

Sonya had a brother named Marco. He was always amazed at how well his sister could draw and paint and fix things. She always wanted things to be pretty. She even wanted Marco to look good, so she would tell him to comb his hair or put on a nicer shirt. Marco got annoyed when his sister did this. But he liked it a little, too.

Sometimes Sonya helped Marco with his arithmetic homework. Mostly, Marco did very well in school. He liked it a lot, and he learned new

skills pretty fast. Math was the only subject that was really hard for him, but Sonya made it easier. She was so good at explaining things. She was like a real teacher even though she was still a kid.

Recently Sonya had helped Marco learn to ride his bicycle. Now he was beginning to get good at bike riding.

Marco admired his big sister. And, most of the time, he and she got along very well. But, like all brothers and sisters, they got angry at each other and argued sometimes.

The Gifts

One day Sonya and Marco's grandparents came for a visit. Both children loved to see their grandmother and grandfather. They were so much fun. And, besides, they usually brought excellent presents.

The grandparents arrived smiling. They

kissed and hugged Sonya and Marco. Their grandfather said, "Marco, you look great in your new glasses. And, Sonya, you look beautiful, as usual."

Their grandmother, of course, handed each child a present. She had brought each of them a book. Marco's book was about dinosaurs, and Sonya's was about dogs. Sonya loved dogs, especially her puppy Chewsy.

Soon the children's aunt and uncle arrived, and everyone sat and talked. "How do you like your new books?" the children's grandmother asked them.

"Super!" Marco piped up. "I've already read five pages of mine. I love it. It's great!"

"And, what about you, Sonya?" her grandmother asked. "Do you like your book?"

"Yes," Sonya said. But really, she hadn't looked at her book at all. Only Chewsy had looked at it. The puppy couldn't wait to sink her teeth into that book.

"Sonya, I hope you'll read that book. It will be good practice for you," her grandmother said.

Marco interrupted them. "I'm a super reader," he said. "You want to hear me read? Let me read for you, Grandma."

"In a minute," his grandmother said. "I'm so glad you're a good reader. Reading is so important. If you read a lot, you'll be a big success when you grow up. Your mother told me you won a prize in your class for reading. We're so proud of you! I used to do well in reading in school, too. You must take after me."

"Can I read to you now, Grandma?" Marco asked. "Then you'll see how good I am."

Sonya looked up and said, "Marco, stop showing off. Grandma doesn't want you to read to her."

Her grandmother then said, "And, Sonya, your mother tells me you're doing a little better in reading in school these days."

"Let's not talk about school," Sonya answered. "It's boring."

Sonya left the room because she felt really bad. Why did her grandmother have to talk about *reading*? Sonya hated reading. She was having a very hard time learning to read.

Everybody at home always talked about how well Marco could read. And he kept bragging about it. That made Sonya feel very, very bad.

Sometimes Sonya felt angry at Marco. She knew this was kind of silly, but she couldn't help it. She felt angry, jealous, and sad all at the same time. Sometimes she wished Marco had a reading problem, too.

An Exciting Bike Trip

Sonya couldn't stop thinking about how bad she had felt in front of her grandmother. Her reading problem made her feel so embarrassed and ashamed. But then the doorbell rang. It was Eddie standing there with his bicycle.

"Hey, Sonya," he said, "want to ride bikes in the park?"

"Great!" Sonya answered. "Where's Becky?"

"She went to the library with Mom. She said you wouldn't want to go 'cause you don't read."

Marco was standing nearby. "Can I go? Can I go with you guys?" he asked.

"No, Marco, you just stay home and read your dumb books," his sister answered. "Eddie and I are really fast at bike riding. You couldn't keep up with us."

Marco looked sad. He really wanted to go bike riding with the older kids. Besides, he thought Eddie was neat. It was always fun to go places with Eddie.

Sonya ran to ask her mother if she could go. Her mother said okay. But she asked Sonya to take Marco, too. Sonya finally said that it would be all right.

As the children left, Marco and Sonya's mother said, "Be home before dark—by 5:30 at the latest. Sonya, you're good at telling time. Wear your watch and make sure you're back on time."

Eddie said, "Marco, you can't take that book with you. It's not safe to read while you ride."

Off went the three kids. Eddie's bike was a real sight. It had ribbons of all colors attached to it. Two old mops were tied to the handlebars. And

a bird cage with a yellow flag on top sat on the back fender.

Eddie said the mops were his bike wings. Birds were supposed to fly in and out of the fender bird cage to give the bike wind power. Eddie told everyone that he had a flycycle, the world's only flying two-wheeler.

Eddie, Sonya, and Marco rode on the sidewalk as they headed toward the park. Eddie was in front, then came Sonya, and finally Marco. He was very far behind. Sonya and Marco's puppy, Chewsy, was all the way in the back.

As Chewsy tried to keep up with the bicycles, she barked and yelped. She was probably trying to tell the kids to slow down so she could catch up.

After a while, Chewsy looked annoyed. She turned and headed back toward home. She decided to work on an important bone chewing project she had started the week before. Plus, she thought she might have a taste of Sonya's new book!

When they got to the park, the kids stopped for a rest. While they were sitting on a big rock, Eddie said, "I'll tell you where we're going. I'm going to show you guys the way to the top-secret giant flying bat caves."

"Caves can't fly," said Sonya.

"Right," answered Eddie, "but *bats* can fly."

"What are giant bat caves?" asked Marco.

"They're old, old, cold, dark, hidden, top-secret underground caves," Eddie explained.

"In the old days, like maybe hundreds of years ago, robbers and pirates and other sly, slimy, sleazy folks used these caves. They used them to hide all the stuff they stole. After these thieves got caught, the treasure just stayed there.

"For a long time, people were afraid to go into the caves. They heard that gigantic, mean attack bats lived there. They thought that these bats flew around in the dark and then swooped down and attacked anyone who came into the caves. It was like the bats were guarding the stolen treasure."

"You mean flying baseball bats?" asked Marco. "You could get hit with *baseball* bats?"

"No, not *baseball* bats!" Eddie answered. "These are bats that look like great, big, huge birds. But they're not really birds—they're bats. Just believe me. I can't explain it.

"Anyway, I found out that these bats are not really so dangerous. They're extremely nice (for bats). And they wake up at night, not during the daytime. They sleep all day. They just hang from the edges of rocks in the dark caves, and they just dream all day—you know, like the way I sometimes dream in class."

"And sometimes you act batty in class," added Sonya.

Eddie then shouted, "Okay, let's get going! We have to get there long before dark. It's much too scary there at night. Besides, our parents want us home on time."

The kids were very excited about their adventure. They thought they might discover some valuable treasure. Eddie pedaled like mad. He turned right, then left, then right, then left again.

"Are we almost there?" panted Marco.

"We'd better be," Sonya said. "It's getting dark. And I just felt a few drops of rain. Eddie, maybe we should start heading back home."

Marco sounded worried when he said, "I think we've been in this same spot before. Are we riding around in circles?"

"Let's see now," Eddie said. "I've never been to these caves before. I've just heard about them. Actually, maybe I've just had a dream about them."

"A dream?" Sonya asked.

"Yeah, a dream, but my dreams are really real. I have true dreams, in true color, with true sounds. Now let's see," Eddie went on. "I'm trying to remember my directions from my dream. You know, I think, I think,—I'm sure—we are definitely lost!"

"Lost?" exclaimed Sonya. "It's getting dark, and now we're lost!"

Marco looked frightened. "Let's go home! Let's go home! This is too scary! What if the attack bats wake up and come flying out at us? I don't want to get hit with a bat even if it's not a baseball bat!"

"Okay," Eddie said, trying to act like the person in charge. "Let's go home. It's raining harder now. We can come back another time. Turn on your batcycle lights. I mean your *bicycle* lights. Let's move it!"

The Accident

The kids started riding as fast as they could. Eddie didn't know where he was going, but he hoped they would end up somewhere good. He often tried to get places fast, so he was used to moving in a big hurry.

Marco was having trouble keeping up with the others. After all, he was just a beginner. He pedaled as fast as he could with his short legs.

Suddenly, Marco tried to slow down to make a turn. His bike skidded off the path and into a tree. As he fell off, his bicycle seemed to fly into the air. Marco landed on the grass, and his bike landed next to him on its side.

Marco yelled for his sister who made a quick turn and headed back toward him. "Are you all right? Are you okay?" she asked.

Luckily, Marco was not hurt at all. He was just a little shaken up. But his new glasses had flown off, and one of the lenses had popped out. Also, the chain had come off his bicycle, so he couldn't ride it.

"Now what are we going to do?" cried Marco.

Even Eddie looked a bit worried. He said,

"We can't leave Marco here. But he can't ride his bike, and he can hardly see without his glasses. We can't take him on our bicycles, either. That wouldn't be safe. And we're getting soaking wet. We are in big, serious trouble!"

Eddie bent down and tried to fix Marco's glasses, but he just couldn't figure out how to do it.

Sonya Saves the Day

Whenever there was a problem, Sonya was good at solving it. She took Marco's glasses and worked on them. Suddenly, they were all fixed.

While Sonya was working on the glasses, Eddie tried to repair Marco's bicycle. Several times he almost had the chain back on, but then it would come off again.

Eddie didn't look closely enough at the chain and the wheel. Instead, he was impulsive (as usual). He worked too fast without really thinking or watching what he was doing.

Finally, Sonya bent down next to the bicycle. She studied the wheel and the chain. At the same time, she looked closely at how the chain is supposed to fit on the wheel. She used her fingers to loosen up a nut on the wheel, and she managed to get the chain back on again. Then she tightened the nut, and the bicycle was all fixed.

"You are super, Sonya!" shouted Eddie. "You are amazing. You are so smart at fixing things. You are so good at figuring out nuts. I'm only good at acting nuts! You are Sonya-the-super-fixer-upper-amazing-cool-genius!"

Sonya said, "I'm more than cool—I'm cold. It's freezing out here! Let's get going."

"Yeah," Eddie answered. "I feel as if I'll be riding a popsicle. If it gets any colder, I'll have the world's first flycycle-icycle-bicycle."

The kids got back on their bikes and rode as

fast as they could. But they didn't know where they were going. They were just plain lost. And they were tired and cold and wet. Marco tried to act brave, but inside he felt like crying.

Home at Last

Finally, the kids saw some lights and a street. They were so glad! As they got closer, it looked very familiar. It was the street that led to Eddie's house! They all felt very lucky.

As soon as they got to Eddie's house, Eddie's father called Marco and Sonya's father. He had begun to worry about the kids. He said he'd be right over to pick them up.

When they got home, Marco told his grandparents all about their big adventure. He told them what Eddie had said about the giant bat caves. Marco said he'd like to go back sometime on a very sunny day so he could get the treasure.

Marco also described his accident. "It was

getting dark then," he said. "You could hardly see. But Sonya figured out how to fix my bicycle *and* my glasses. She was fantastic. Eddie called her Sonya-the-amazing-cool-genius-upper-fixer— or something like that."

Sonya felt so proud. Then she looked over at the book her grandparents had brought her. It was lying on the table. Sonya didn't say anything, but she wondered how she could be so good at doing some things and so bad at other things. How could it be so easy for her to fix things but so hard for her to read?

Sonya's Learning Disorder

Sonya had always wanted to read. She loved listening to stories, and she liked the pictures in books. Beginning in first grade, Sonya's teachers kept trying to teach her to read. But Sonya couldn't seem to do it.

That was because Sonya had a **reading**

disorder. Sonya's mother told her that her reading disorder is sometimes called **dyslexia**. Sonya had a hard time even pronouncing that word.

Most of the other children in Sonya's class were reading pretty well. But Sonya just couldn't remember what sounds go with what letters when she looked at letters in words.

Her teacher, Mrs. Grillo, would show Sonya some letters like *ck* or *ike*. Then Mrs. Grillo would say the sound that those letters make in a word. Sonya would repeat the sound. She could remember it for a little while. But when Sonya would see the letters a few days later, or even the next day, she just could not remember their sound. Sonya had so much trouble remembering what sounds go with what letters.

One day Mrs. Grillo put *fr* on the board. She spoke very slowly as she said, "*fr* sounds like /frrr/ as in *from*. Sonya, can you say /frrr/ as in *from*?"

Sonya answered, "Yes, /frrr/."

Mrs. Grillo said, "That's perfect, Sonya! Now try to remember it."

The next day, Mrs. Grillo put *fr* on the board, but Sonya just could not remember the sound that the letters *fr* make.

It was a little easier for Sonya to remember the sound of one letter alone—like *m*.

Sometimes Sonya even had trouble saying a

word after Mrs. Grillo said it, unless Mrs. Grillo said the word sounds very slowly.

Sonya's Learning Disabilities Teacher

In school, Sonya had a **learning disabilities teacher**, Mr. Nasser. He gave Sonya some extra help with her reading. Sonya would see him in another classroom three times a week. Two other children who were also having reading problems got help with Sonya.

Sometimes Sonya felt ashamed when she went for extra help. Derek, a boy in her class, made her feel very bad one day. As Sonya was leaving to go see Mr. Nasser, Derek said, "Good-bye, Sonya, have fun in the mental room." Some of the other kids laughed. Sonya felt awful.

One day Mr. Nasser explained that everyone's mind has to think about sounds. He told the students that thinking about sounds is important for listening, for reading, and for spelling.

He said that as soon as a person's ears hear a sound, that sound goes right into the person's mind. Then the mind decides whether the sound is a car horn, a whistle, or a friend saying something.

Mr. Nasser also explained that word sounds come into a person's mind very, very quickly. They also leave fast. So, a mind has to work very fast when it figures out word sounds. Figuring out word sounds is one of the fastest things a mind has to do.

Mr. Nasser said that while you're listening to someone your mind needs to remember the special sounds that go together to make words. For example, a person's mind is supposed to tell the difference between word sounds that are almost the same—in words like *shoe* and *show*.

Word sounds were very hard for Sonya. She had the hardest time when she tried to get word sounds to go with the letters in words. That kind of mind work really confused her.

Mr. Nasser said that it was not easy for Sonya to **decode** words. He explained that the words on a page are like a secret code. The letters and the sounds they make stand for ideas or things. If you can't figure out all the sounds in the reading code, you may miss the ideas that the words are trying to tell you while you read.

Sonya could see the letters in words. She just couldn't get them to stand for the right sounds in her memory. She couldn't decode the words well.

Sonya also had big problems with spelling. She could remember a little bit about how words look, but she couldn't seem to get all the right letters into words.

Sometimes, when she tried to spell, Sonya would get the first letter right in a word, but then she couldn't get the rest of the word. Sometimes she could get the first letter and the last letter right, but she would forget what went in the middle.

Mr. Nasser also said that some people are

born with the kind of mind that has trouble with word sounds. This is not their fault, and it doesn't mean that they are dumb. But sometimes it makes them *feel* very dumb. They shouldn't feel dumb, however—lots of very smart people have trouble with word sounds.

Short Words, Long Words, and Sentences

Mr. Nasser gave Sonya lots of practice at decoding. Little by little, she got faster at seeing some letters in groups and figuring out what sounds go with those letters. She started to get pretty good with short words. She could even spell some of them.

But it was still very hard for Sonya to read whole words, especially long ones. In a long word, Sonya would figure out the first sound, and then figure out the second sound, but then while she was figuring out the third sound, she would forget the first sound. This made it very tough for her to put the whole word together again in her mind.

Parts of a word would keep disappearing from Sonya's mind. It was like a TV screen that couldn't show a whole picture. Often Sonya would figure out one part of a word and then guess the rest of it. Sometimes she'd be right, but a lot of times she was wrong.

When Sonya tried to read whole sentences, she sometimes knew a few words. These were usually short words like *run* or *boy*. She would have to use these little words to guess what the rest of the words probably were.

One time, Sonya was supposed to read the sentence *Cats climb up trees*. She could figure out the words *cats* and *trees*, but she couldn't decode the word *climb*. At first, she thought it was *clown*. But then she remembered that cats *climb* trees, so she decided that the word was probably not *clown* but *climb*.

Even though Sonya could figure out some

words by guessing or using hints, she still made many mistakes. And her reading was much too slow.

Sonya Feels Ashamed and Sad

Every student had to do some reading in front of the class. When it was her turn, Sonya was always afraid. She felt so ashamed when she tried to read out loud.

Sometimes a few of the other kids would laugh at Sonya's slow reading and all her mistakes. There was one boy named Bill who always tried to act tough. He and Derek sometimes laughed when Sonya tried to read.

Sonya had lots of friends. Her best friend was Eddie's sister Becky. Another friend, of course, was her puppy Chewsy who followed her almost everywhere. Chewsy was the first one to greet Sonya when she came home from school. She would wait for Sonya to get off the bus and then she would bark hello. Sonya once said to her mother that Chewsy was the only one who didn't care whether she could read.

One day Sonya told her mother that she didn't even *want* to read or spell. She said she hated reading, that reading was boring. She said she was starting to hate school, that her teacher was mean, and that she was the worst student in her class. Sonya also said that sometimes she couldn't stand her brother Marco because he could read and she couldn't.

Sonya's parents tried to tell her that she was really smart. They said she had to be smart to be so good at arithmetic and so super at helping Marco with it. She also had to be smart to be so good at fixing things like eyeglasses and bicycles.

Sonya's father reminded her that she liked all sports and always had fun in gym. She was excellent at drawing, and she loved her art class in school. He told her she just couldn't give up too quickly when it came to reading. And she couldn't let her reading problem spoil the other parts of school for her. Sonya knew her father was right.

A Book about Bat Caves

One Saturday, Sonya went to the telephone and called Eddie. "Eddie," she said, "can we get our bikes and go look for those flying bat caves again? You and Marco and I? We're probably the only people in the world who know about them. I think we should find those caves and then write a story or a whole book about the giant, secret, flying bat caves—or whatever you call them."

"A story? A book?" Eddie asked, surprised. "I thought you hated books."

"I'm starting to like books better. I mean I'm trying to start to like books better," said Sonya. "Here's what we'll do: you can think up the story and write the story, and I'll draw all the pictures."

"But it's too hard for people to read my messy handwriting," Eddie shouted over the phone. "Wait a minute. I know what we can do. Marco and Becky can help us. I'll think up the far out ideas about what we saw—or think we saw— at the secret, flying bat caves. Becky can write down the ideas. You can draw the pictures. And Marco can check out the spelling."

"That sounds excellent!" Sonya said.

Eddie laughed. "It'll be super. Everyone will want to read our book. And we'll be called the Bike Rider Writers, the world's most famous writing team. I'll go get Becky, and we'll be right over—ready to ride right and write right!"

4. Bill's Kind of Mind

Bill thought cars were the greatest things.
He knew all about them. One day in class,
he explained how car engines work. He drew
pictures on the board to show how gasoline gets
used by an engine to make a car's wheels turn.
He also drew some pictures of cars of the future.
He said that someday cars might even be able to
run on sun and wind power.

Eddie asked Bill if these cars would be able
to use wind power when it was windy, sun power

when it was sunny, rain power when it rained, and moon power at night. Bill said that would be cool. He got so excited when he talked about cars. And everyone was surprised at how much he knew about them.

Bill was also a star in physical education. His team almost always won—no matter what the sport was. Everyone wanted Bill on their team. He got along really well with other kids when he was playing a sport.

But Bill seemed like a totally different person when it came to other parts of school. When he was not thinking about cars or playing a sport, he had serious problems. He had trouble learning and big trouble getting along with other kids.

Bill wasn't doing well at all in Mrs. Grillo's class. He was having problems in every subject. Often, he didn't have time to finish his work. Plus, he would forget to do things that he was supposed to do.

Whenever Bill's mother or father talked to

him about his problems in school, he would insist he didn't have any. Every once in a while, Bill would get really angry. Once he said to his mother, "Just leave me alone! There's nothing wrong with me. I'll do okay if everyone stops bugging me about my schoolwork."

A Wallet Is Missing

Sometimes Bill got into trouble in school. One time he got into *serious* trouble. Here's what happened:

Just as everyone was about to go to the cafeteria for lunch, Becky got very upset. She went up to Mrs. Grillo and said, "I can't find my wallet! I've lost my wallet! What should I do?"

Mrs. Grillo answered, "Well, look around. I'm sure it's here somewhere. Did you look in your desk? Did you search through your backpack?"

Becky was practically crying now. "I've looked everywhere. I've looked everywhere!"

Mrs. Grillo told Becky to go back and look again. A few minutes later, Becky returned. She told Mrs. Grillo she still couldn't find her wallet. She said it had some other important things in it besides her lunch money.

It contained pictures of her whole family. "I love those pictures," Becky said. "I don't want to lose the pictures of my father and mother and our dog Hot Fudge. I even have a picture of Eddie, but I guess I don't mind losing that one."

Mrs. Grillo lent Becky some money to buy lunch. After the children returned to class, Mrs. Grillo asked them all to look around for Becky's missing wallet. No one could find it anywhere.

Suddenly Bill said, "I bet Eddie took his sister's wallet. He's always doing stuff like that. He takes things without thinking."

That made Eddie mad. "I didn't take her

wallet! I'm not a thief! Maybe *you* stole it, Bill. Or, maybe Becky dropped it into the deep, creepy pit where Wally-the-Wallet-Eating-Wallaby lives."

The Wallet Is Found

When school was almost over that day, Mrs. Grillo told everyone to clean up. She said, "Make sure that everything inside your desks is neat."

All the children began to clean their desks, all except Eddie. He said his desk was too messy to clean. He said it was his private black hole junk dump, and it would take him weeks to figure out where to put all the junk he had collected. (Eddie loved to save everything he found. A lot of it went into his room at home and his desk in school.) But then he changed his mind. He decided to do his best to fix up his junk dump— at least a little.

Then, as usual, Eddie started minding everyone else's business. He sat next to Bill, and he watched Bill cleaning out his desk, too. At times like this, Eddie forgot to watch what he was doing himself.

All of a sudden, Eddie noticed something red in Bill's desk. It was a red leather wallet. Eddie shouted, "You thief! You robber! You said *I* did it, but *you* stole my sister's wallet!"

Eddie grabbed the wallet from Bill's desk. He held it up in the air for everyone to see.

Bill said very loudly, "I didn't take it. I don't know how it got here. Becky must have put it in my desk."

Becky came and grabbed the wallet from Eddie. She said to Bill, "You're a liar! I know you stole my wallet!"

"I didn't steal it," Bill replied. "I found it on the floor. I knew it must belong to someone around here. I was just saving it. I was going to give it back."

Mrs. Grillo came over and told the children to stop arguing. "Take your wallet, Becky, and

let's not discuss it anymore right now," she said. "And, Eddie, why don't you calm down? It's time to go home."

Mrs. Grillo Talks with Bill

As the children were leaving the classroom, Mrs. Grillo said to Bill, "Bill, may I talk to you for a second?"

Bill stopped at Mrs. Grillo's desk, but he did not say a word. He just looked down at the floor.

"Bill," Mrs. Grillo said, "I need you to be very honest with me. I think you *did* take Becky's wallet. If you did, I'd like you to admit it. It's very important for you to tell me the truth."

Bill looked very upset. "I didn't take it! I didn't! I'm telling the truth!" Mrs. Grillo could see that Bill was starting to cry.

"Why do I always get blamed for everything?" asked Bill.

"You don't get blamed for everything, Bill.

But you do get into a lot of trouble, and you always say it's not your fault."

Bill then said, "Okay, so what if I took the wallet? You can punish me. You can kick me out of school. They can put me in jail. I don't care. I don't care what happens to me. Just don't tell my mom or dad."

Mrs. Grillo said, "Bill, why do you keep getting into trouble? Why do you act tough so often? Why do you have to get into so many fights with other kids?"

Bill answered, "I hate school. I hate this class. Anyway, nobody lets me have fun anymore."

Mrs. Grillo said, "Bill, I wish you'd start trying to like school. You could contribute so much to our class. You always come up with such excellent ideas when we have discussions.

"You know more about cars than anyone else. Remember how you explained the way a car's engine works to the other children? I can tell that you're real smart, Bill."

Bill replied, "No way. That's a joke. I'm not smart. I'm the stupidest kid in the class. I'm the class dumbhead. Everyone else can learn things, but I can't.

"The only stuff I can learn is car stuff. In class, I can't remember anything. I can't remember things I read in books. I can't remember vocabulary words. I can't even learn my facts in arithmetic!"

Mrs. Grillo then said, "Bill, you *are* smart. It's just that you have trouble remembering certain kinds of things."

"Yeah, maybe," Bill admitted. "But now I'm in real trouble at home, too."

"Why? What's going on at home?" Mrs. Grillo asked.

Bill could hardly speak because he was so sad. "My dad says I can't play soccer anymore because my last report card was so bad. He says I can't play soccer until I get better marks and start behaving myself in school.

"I hate school. It's boring. And I love soccer. It's the one thing I'm good at. My dad's the coach, and he won't even let me play!"

Mrs. Grillo said, "Bill, I need to have a talk with your mother and father."

Bill began to plead. "Please, Mrs. Grillo. Please, Mrs. Grillo. Don't tell them I took Becky's wallet! They'll kill me. They won't let me out of my room. They'll be so mad at me. I'll never get to play soccer again. Don't tell them! Don't tell them! I'll never forgive you if you say anything to them. Don't tell them anything!"

"I have to tell them, Bill. They need to know about your problems. And, you have to learn that you can't get away with things like taking Becky's wallet."

Bill Goes Home

Bill ran out of the room and headed towards the school bus. He got on and didn't talk to anyone all the way home. One of the kids called Bill a crook. Someone else said he belonged in jail. Bill didn't say a word. In his whole life, he had never felt so sad—and so scared.

Bill didn't say a word when he got home, either. He went straight to his bedroom, put his head in his pillow, and started to cry. His dog Napper started to cry, too. Napper could always tell when Bill was sad, and he hated to see Bill unhappy.

Napper got his name because he loved to take naps. He had excellent sleeping skills. He also had exciting dog dreams. You could tell by the way he growled or made squeaking sounds when he was sleeping.

While Bill was in his bedroom, he heard the telephone ring. His mother answered it and seemed to be talking for a long time.

Bill said to himself, "I bet that's Mrs. Grillo. I bet she's telling Mom all about how I took Becky's wallet. I'm in real trouble now. I feel horrible. I'm so scared. Why did I do it? Why did I take it? I feel so mixed up!"

Bill's cat, Cool Cat, jumped up on the back of his neck and purred loudly. Napper started to lick Bill's tears. But soon Napper fell asleep with his head against the side of Bill's face. Bill was thinking that his dog and cat were the only ones that cared about him.

Then Bill's mother came into the room. He could guess what she was going to say.

"Bill," his mother began, "that was Mrs. Grillo. She told me what happened in school today. I couldn't believe my ears.

"This is it. You've been in so much trouble in school this year. Mrs. Grillo says your behavior's been pretty bad. Plus, she says that you haven't been doing your work lately. She must think you're a troublemaker. She must think your father and I are awful parents."

Bill didn't say a thing. He wouldn't look at his mother.

"At this rate," she said, "you'll *never* be allowed to play soccer again."

Bill looked up and said, "I don't care. Just leave me alone. Leave me alone with Napper and Cool Cat." Napper was now on his back with his feet in the air. He was making little squeaks. He must have been having a musical dream.

Finally, Bill looked up at his mother and said, "Mom, I'm mad. I'm mad at everyone. No one ever says anything good about me. I was born to fail. I'm a loser, a total loser."

"That's not true, that's not true," said Bill's mother. "You know how much your father and I love you. We want to be proud of you. We want you to get along with other kids and do good work in school.

"I'm sure you could do well if only you'd really try. If only you'd settle down, you could be great in soccer *and* in school. The first thing you need to do is to start behaving."

"That's not so easy," Bill said.

Bill's mother answered, "I know it's not easy, Bill. For some reason, you feel you *have* to act cool and tough in school.

"Sometimes I think you get into trouble so that other kids won't notice that you have learning problems. You're so afraid they'll think you're dumb or something. Maybe you've decided that it's less embarrassing or easier to be a behavior problem."

Bill was quiet at first, but then he looked up and said, "Please go away. Just leave me and Napper and Cool Cat alone."

His mother left the room, but Bill thought very hard about what she had just said.

Bill Gets Tested

That evening when Bill's father came home, his parents had a long talk about Bill. The next day, they called Mrs. Grillo. Everyone agreed that Bill should visit the **school psychologist**, Dr. Silva.

Dr. Silva knew how to test kids to find out their strengths and weaknesses. She also knew how to use tests to learn more about why kids behave the way they do.

In a few days, Bill went to take the tests. He didn't want to, but he went anyway. Dr. Silva was very nice. During many parts of the tests, she told Bill how well he was doing. That surprised him.

First, Dr. Silva gave Bill an **IQ test**. She

explained that an IQ test is an **intelligence test**. It tests your mind to help find out about your strengths and weaknesses. Also, it shows how easy or hard it is for you to do different kinds of mind work.

On the IQ test there were puzzles, pencil games, questions about all kinds of things, and tests of how well you remember.

Bill had to put together a few puzzles while Dr. Silva watched. He was very fast at doing these. For one of the puzzles, Bill had to make some designs with blocks. It was fun, and Bill did a great job. Dr. Silva said that Bill did the puzzles as well as most older kids.

Dr. Silva also asked Bill some questions about all different kinds of things. She later said that she was testing Bill's understanding or **comprehension**. Bill found this part of the IQ test extremely easy. It showed how well he understood things when people talked to him. But some other parts of the test were hard for Bill.

On one section of the test, Dr. Silva read a list of numbers. She read one number at a time. Then Bill had to repeat the numbers in the same order that Dr. Silva had said them.

For example, Dr. Silva said, "4, 3, 1, 6."

Bill repeated, "4, 1, 3, 6."

Then Dr. Silva said, "8, 2, 5, 3, 1."

Bill said, "8, 2, 1, 3." He forgot one of the numbers. He also mixed up the order of some numbers.

On this part of the test, Bill kept on leaving out numbers or forgetting their order.

Another section of the test gave Bill some trouble, too. It was a game where you had to look at a picture and figure out what was missing. It was difficult for Bill because he had to *remember* what things looked like.

Bill also had a hard time answering questions about facts you were supposed to know. He kept thinking he sort of knew the answers, but it was hard for him to remember them.

Dr. Silva then gave Bill some **achievement tests**. She explained that achievement tests are used to find out how well you have learned different skills like reading and math.

The tests showed that Bill could look at words and read them out loud very well. That meant his **decoding skills** were good. He could also read and understand paragraphs, so he had good **comprehension**.

But Bill had big problems with the kind of

mind work needed for writing and arithmetic. Recently, his class had started learning the multiplication tables. They were much too hard for Bill to remember.

He understood how multiplication works, but he couldn't remember math facts like how much 8×4 is. Even when he studied, it was hard for him to remember math facts.

Next, Dr. Silva asked Bill to write a short paragraph. She noticed that he made some of his letters the wrong way and his writing was pretty messy. He made a lot of spelling mistakes. Also, he forgot to capitalize a name and a word at the beginning of a sentence.

While he was busy writing, Bill would forget how to capitalize and how to make certain letters. He would also forget how to spell words he usually *could* spell. It seemed as if there were too many things to remember at once. He usually could remember one thing at a time, but not many things all at once.

What Bill Found Out from Dr. Silva

A few days later, Dr. Silva spent some time telling Bill and his parents how he had done on the tests. She told everyone about Bill's strengths.

She talked about his good reading skills. She told them how well he had done on some parts of the IQ test. Bill felt proud. He could tell that Dr. Silva did not think that he was stupid.

Then Dr. Silva brought up Bill's problems. This made him nervous. At first, he didn't want to hear about his problems. He didn't want his parents to find out about them either.

He stared out the window and pretended he wasn't really listening. He wished Napper and Cool Cat were with him. They didn't think he was a problem kid. He looked at his watch for a little while. Then he started playing with his belt buckle. He wanted his parents to think he didn't care. He tried to act bored.

Dr. Silva said, "Bill, I know it's hard to hear about your weaknesses, but please try to listen. Everyone has strengths, and everyone has weaknesses.

"There are no perfect kinds of minds. There are many kinds of mind work that *my* mind cannot do well. There are a lot of things that your father's and mother's minds are not good at. It's only human to have strengths and weaknesses."

Dr. Silva then said, "Bill, you have some learning disorders. They are not real bad, but they're bad enough to cause trouble when you try to learn in school. You seem to have a problem with your memory.

"You're not so good at remembering some of the things you need to remember for school. You are much better at *understanding* facts or ideas than you are at *remembering* them.

"You know, Bill," Dr. Silva continued, "a person's mind has many different kinds of memory work to do. Everyone's mind is good at doing some kinds of memory work and not so good at other kinds of memory work.

"You are great at remembering how to do things with your body. That's one reason you're so excellent at soccer. You're also good at remembering how to decode words when you read. And you can remember all about cars."

Dr. Silva explained that on the tests Bill's mind had a lot of trouble doing some of the kinds of memory work you need for school. He had real problems with something called **sequencing**. Sequencing means remembering things in the correct order. She reminded Bill that it was hard for him to repeat the list of numbers she read to him during the IQ test.

It was also hard for Bill to remember the order of the days in the week and the order of months in the year. Telling time was a problem, too, because time is full of sequences. Bill was often mixed up about time.

Remembering several things at once was another problem for Bill. That's why it was so hard for him to write well. He had good ideas. But while he was trying to remember how to form the letters on a page, he would forget his ideas. Or he would forget about spelling and punctuation rules while he was trying to make his letters look neat.

Bill's writing was often an embarrassing mess. To write well, you have to have very good memory ability. Bill's poor memory for writing kept ruining his writing.

Dr. Silva told Bill that a mind is like a huge dresser with drawers in it. You have to put ideas and facts and even new skills into your mind's "drawers" so you can store them there and find them later when you need them.

When Bill had to remember spelling or math

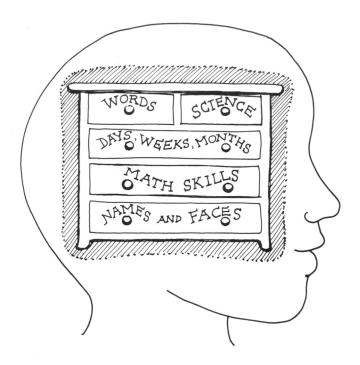

facts, he couldn't find them in his "memory drawers." That made it hard for him to remember what he needed when he took a test or when he had to answer a question in class.

Dr. Silva also explained that Bill did a lot of his work too slowly because it took him so long to remember things. That's why he always seemed to need more time on tests.

"Dr. Silva is right," Bill thought. "I do have a problem remembering. My mind gets my muscles to remember everything for sports but not for writing. I just can't *remember* some school stuff, even when it's easy for me to *understand* it."

Bill looked up and said, "I really do try. I *try* to learn. I understand most things. I just can't remember well."

Then Bill asked, "But will my memory problems go away? Will I get all better?"

Dr. Silva answered, "Honestly, Bill, I don't know. You may always have a little trouble remembering certain things. But I do know your memory will improve a lot if we all work on it together. If you give up, or if you pretend you have no problems, your memory might even get worse."

Bill asked, "How can I work on it?"

"It's really just like trying to get better at soccer," Dr. Silva said. "Your soccer coach might tell you what you need to do to build up some of your leg muscles to kick harder or run faster. Then you'd have to keep on practicing and practicing to strengthen those muscles. It's the same with memory. You need to find out what exercises to do to make your memory stronger. Then you need to practice using your memory for school. Memory exercises are sometimes called **strategies**."

Bill laughed as he thought about his memory as if it were a kind of muscle. "I guess I'll have to learn about those strategies so I can get strong memory muscles!" Bill said.

Dr. Silva told Bill and his parents that she would soon have a meeting with Mrs. Grillo and the principal and some other people who knew about learning disorders. Together they would make up an **educational plan**. It would explain how everyone could help Bill at school and at home.

Bill started to feel better than he had felt at the beginning of the meeting. As soon as they got home, Bill said to his father, "Now, can I play soccer?"

"No, not yet," said his father.

Bill couldn't believe his ears. "Why can't I play soccer? It's not fair! You're punishing me because I have a learning disorder. It isn't my fault that I can't find some things in my mind's memory drawers. It's not fair! How can you punish me for my problem by not letting me play soccer?"

"Your father's not punishing you, Bill," his mother said. "You have to prove to us that you really *are trying* to help your memory, to write better, and to do better in math.

"We also want to see a big change in your behavior. When we feel you are really trying, we'll think about letting you play soccer again."

That didn't make Bill feel any better. He wondered if he really could fix up his memory. He knew practice could make him better at soccer, but he wondered whether practice would ever make him good at remembering.

Bill Gets Help

Bill started to get some help from Ms. Laski, a special teacher in school. At first, he was a little ashamed to get help. He remembered how he used to make fun of Sonya when *she* went for extra help in school. But he realized he definitely needed to get better at some kinds of remembering.

Ms. Laski taught Bill more about his memory. She also taught him how to use different memory strategies. She told Bill that when he needed to remember something important while he was reading, he could try to whisper the idea to himself. He could also try to make a picture of the idea in his mind. She said he could try to make lists or draw little pictures of what he wanted to remember.

Ms. Laski told Bill he should test himself when he was trying to learn something that he would have to remember later. She said he had to make a plan to do this. She taught him how to make flash cards for the multiplication tables. On one side of a card, he would write something like $4 \times 9 = ?$ On the other side of the same card, he would write the correct answer (36).

As Bill memorized, he could test himself with the cards. Whenever he got one right, he could remove it from the stack. Ms. Laski said Bill could even make up games and score points for remembering math facts.

Bill also got help with some of the memory problems that were making it hard for him to write well. Instead of trying to remember many things at the same time, he learned to work in steps.

- First, he thought up ideas and talked them into a tape recorder.
- Then, he listened to his tape and wrote down the best or the most important ideas

on little cards. He put only one idea on each card.

- Next, he put these cards in the best order.
- After that, he used the cards to put his ideas on paper without worrying about writing neatly or carefully.
- Finally, he fixed up things like spelling, capitalization, and punctuation.

Bill also started to use the family's computer for school work. His father said it would be a big help with writing. He told Bill that having a computer was like having extra memory drawers. Bill had always liked the computer for playing games, but now he also wanted to use it to work on his writing.

Mrs. Grillo helped Bill, too. He was always afraid of being called on in class. It usually took him too long to remember answers.

To help Bill each day, Mrs. Grillo would tell him the question she would ask him the next day.

Then, Bill could think about the question at home before school. That gave him more remembering time.

Sometimes Bill was allowed to use a calculator when he did arithmetic. That gave him less memory mind work to do.

Other times, Mrs. Grillo told Bill he did not have to do all the problems on an arithmetic test. That gave him more time to remember his arithmetic facts.

Bill Does Better

After three weeks, Mrs. Grillo called Bill's parents to say that he was doing much better in school. He was handing in all his assignments. His behavior had improved, too.

After that phone conversation, Bill's mother said to him, "You used to think you were dumb. Now you understand yourself better. You know you are really smart, but you have a learning disorder.

"You can understand things very well; you just have trouble remembering. But your memory is already improving. Mrs. Grillo says there are a lot of new things you can do. She says you can feel your memory getting stronger. It is still a problem, but the problem is not as bad as it was."

The Championship Game

By now, there was only one game left in the soccer season. Bill went to his father and said, "Dad, now that I'm doing better in school, can I play soccer? Please, can I play soccer? I want to play in the last game, the championship game. It's tomorrow!"

Bill's father said, "Bill, I'm really sorry, but I told you that you would probably be out for the rest of the season. I said I'd have to see your next report card before you could play again. And your next report card doesn't come out for another ten days. I'm really sorry. You won't be able to play in the championship game, but why don't you come along and watch?"

Bill was sad and angry. He shouted at his father, "I've worked so hard! And now you won't let me play. Why are you always so nice to my brother and so mean to me?"

"I'm not being mean," Bill father's said. "I'm trying to help you. You'll thank me for this some day."

Bill ran out of the room, but the next day he did go to see the game. He even wore his uniform, although he knew he couldn't play.

He sat down at the end of the bench with his dog Napper on his lap. He didn't talk to anybody. He couldn't even talk to Napper because Napper was sound asleep, even with the noise of all the kids shouting.

Bill's mother always came to the games. But,

she got to this one about fifteen minutes late. When she arrived, she went up to Bill's father and whispered something in his ear. Bill's father smiled.

The other team had scored 3 goals in the first half. They were winning 3 to 1. There were now 7 minutes left in the game.

Bill's father walked over to Bill and put his arm around him. "Congratulations, Bill," he said. "Your mother just got a phone call from Mrs. Grillo. She said your next report card will be much better than the last one.

"It looks as if you really *have* been working on your memory and also your behavior. Now let's see if you still remember how to play soccer. Why don't you go out there and score us some goals?"

Bill couldn't believe his ears. He ran out onto the field. Napper woke up and got excited. His tail wagged so fast you could hardly see it. He gave a barking cheer for Bill. He was so happy he couldn't even fall asleep again.

In two minutes, Bill had scored a big goal. The score was now 3 to 2.

Then Bill took the ball down the field and made a great pass to Eve. She kicked the ball into the net, so the score was tied.

With less than one minute to go, Bill brought the ball out into the center of the field. He looked one way and kicked the ball toward the goal. The goalie fell to the ground and just managed to tip the ball out of the net.

The game ended in a tie. Bill was so disappointed! He wanted his team to win the championship. Instead, it turned out to be a tie game—two teams were the champions.

Bill's father was very pleased with how Bill had done. Napper yawned, but he seemed proud of Bill, too. He kept licking Bill's cheeks and nose.

Bill's father said, "You were great! We would

have lost the game without you. It's too bad we didn't win, but now we have something to work on for next season. It's like your memory. You can't fix it all at once. You have to keep working on it. You have to keep improving."

Bill and his parents and Napper drove home together. Napper remembered that he had forgotten to take his afternoon nap. That was unusual because Napper's kind of mind almost

never forgot when it was time to sleep. Sleeping was his favorite kind of mind work! So, soon he was fast asleep, and it sounded as if there were two engines roaring and snoring along the highway.

All the way home, Bill and his parents talked about the game. Bill's father asked, "What was the score again?"

Bill answered, "What's the matter, Dad?" Do *you* have some kind of a memory problem?"

"Bill," he said, "I've always understood things better than I've remembered them."

"Oh, I see," said Bill. "I think it was 4 to 4."

5. Eve's Kind of Mind

Eve couldn't stand to see anyone unhappy. When anyone or anything suffered, she felt so sad.

One day at school, some kids were standing in the hall. One boy noticed a large spider web just above his locker. This boy took his pencil, reached up as high as he could, and destroyed the web. The spider tried to hold on to one last thread, but he couldn't and he fell to the ground. As the boy's friends jumped away from the running spider, the boy laughed. "Don't worry, you guys," he said. "I'll crush it like a pancake!"

Eve was standing nearby, and she saw what was happening. She ran over and said, "Please don't kill it! Don't hurt it. Um . . . leave it alone."

The boy who was going to crush the spider just shrugged his shoulders and headed off to class with his friends.

Eve bent down to look at the spider, who must have been very frightened. She took a piece of paper out of her notebook and let the spider crawl onto it. Then she put the spider on top of some shelves. "Don't worry," she said softly. "You can make a new web house. They won't try to hurt you anymore."

It's not surprising that everyone liked Eve. She really cared about other people. She remembered her friends' birthdays and reminded Mrs. Grillo when a classmate's birthday was coming up. She was always willing to help out with things. She worked harder than anyone else

at decorating the school for holidays. She
enjoyed trying to make the other kids happy.

Still, nobody really knew Eve very well. She
was so quiet. In class, she talked only when Mrs.
Grillo asked her a question. A lot of the time, she
seemed mixed up or confused. Often, she looked
as if she didn't understand things too well.

Eve's parents noticed that she didn't like to
talk in long sentences. When Eve's father would
ask her what she had done in school, Eve would

answer, "Stuff." Or if her mother asked, "How was school today?" Eve would answer, "Okay." She never liked to give long descriptions.

A Problem with Understanding

Both Mrs. Grillo and Eve's parents were concerned about her. They knew she was having a lot of trouble understanding things in school.

It was hard for Eve to understand what she read. Sometimes she also had trouble understanding what people were explaining to her. She would get mixed up when Mrs. Grillo talked in long or complicated sentences. When Mrs. Grillo said several things in a row, Eve missed some of them. But the other children seemed to understand Mrs. Grillo. That made Eve feel different. "How come *everyone else* understands?" she wondered. "What's the matter with *my* mind?"

Eve had trouble with many subjects in school

because of her problem with understanding. She found subjects like science very difficult. In science lessons, Mrs. Grillo's explanations were often complicated. When Eve couldn't understand them, she might just stop listening. This was because it was hard for her to keep listening when she was confused. Instead, she would daydream or look out the window—the way Eddie did. (But Eddie *could* understand. He "tuned out" because it was hard for him to pay attention.)

Problems with Speaking and Writing

When Eve tried to talk, she sometimes had trouble thinking of the right words for her ideas. She also had trouble saying sentences that sounded right. Other kids found it so much easier to put their ideas into words.

It was also easier for other kids to write about their ideas. Eve had trouble putting her ideas into writing because it was hard for her to think of the right words and make good sentences.

Eve's problems made her sad and scared. She was afraid that other kids would think she was dumb. She tried to be very quiet in class so that no one would notice that she was having trouble.

Eve Disappears

Some days at school were especially scary for Eve. These were the days when there was a lot she could not understand. One Friday, she became very, very discouraged.

Mrs. Grillo had given the children a test that day, and Eve could not understand some of the questions. She had to guess at them. She could tell that she hadn't done very well on the test.

On the same day, Mrs. Grillo went over some homework everyone had done the night before. Eve hadn't been able to understand what she was supposed to do. She had been too embarrassed to ask Mrs. Grillo in class on Thursday. That Friday afternoon Eve disappeared.

She was last seen on the bus. As usual, Eve had been dropped off at the corner near her house. Later on, the other children said they had not seen where Eve had gone. They said she hadn't said anything to them about going anywhere special.

In fact, as usual, Eve didn't say much at all on the trip home from school. She never said very much to anyone. Kids thought she was shy.

When Eve's mother came home from work, she could tell that Eve was missing. She looked in the backyard where Eve often played with her dog Barktalk.

Barktalk got his name because he loved to bark so much. He would bark out all his ideas, and it sounded as if he was speaking a very special dog language. He always found a lot to barktalk about.

Eve's mother checked the backyard, but Barktalk was alone lying under a tree. There was no sign of Eve. Eve's mother looked all over the house and kept calling, "Eve!" but there was no answer. Barktalk could tell that Eve was missing, so he made some nervous bark calls.

Eve's mother called the parents of the other children in Eve's class, and she also called the neighbors. No one, no one at all, had seen Eve. Eve's mother was beginning to feel frantic.

By then, Eve's father had arrived home from work, too. At about the same time, Eve's older sister Judy came back from playing soccer. She got very upset when she found out Eve was missing. "Call the police! Call the police right away!" she cried.

Eve's parents talked about what to do. Then her father went to the phone and called the police. They said that they would send out a radio message to their police cars who would help search for Eve.

A police officer came to the house and asked a lot of questions about where Eve might be. The officer also wanted to talk with some of the other children in Eve's class and to the bus driver. Just before she left, the police officer asked Eve's mother, "By the way, has anything been bothering Eve lately?"

Eve's mother answered, "I don't think so. I don't really know. You see, Eve is very quiet. She keeps everything inside herself. It's hard to know when she is happy and when she is sad."

"Well, has anything happened *lately* to upset her?" asked the officer.

Eve's mother thought about this question and

then answered, "Well, you know, she has a very hard time in school. She really doesn't like school at all."

"I'm afraid that information won't help us find her," answered the officer.

Eve's mother became more and more upset. Her voice shook as she said, "I hope she's all right. I hope nothing has happened to her."

Everyone Worries about Eve

By early that evening, many of the children in Eve's class knew that she was missing. Some of them offered to go out and help find their classmate. Everyone was upset.

Eddie said that he would get all their dogs together to go out sniffing for Eve. Eddie seemed to be the kid who was most concerned about Eve. He cared about other people a lot.

Barktalk joined the search for Eve at home, too. He sniffed all over the house as he looked for his best friend. He even checked under the bed. He ran back and forth from the front door to the back door to bark for Eve.

Eve's mother called Mrs. Grillo to find out if Eve had said or done anything unusual in school that day. Mrs. Grillo said that, as usual, Eve had been very quiet. Mrs. Grillo also remembered that Eve had failed a test she had taken that day.

The test was on one part of a science book the class was supposed to be reading. Mrs. Grillo also said that Eve had forgotten to do her arithmetic homework. Otherwise, nothing unusual had happened.

Then Mrs. Grillo thought some more and said that Eve seemed to be very sad lately. Something seemed to be bothering her.

While everyone kept wondering what had happened to Eve, the police searched all over town. But they couldn't find Eve anywhere. That evening, the television and radio stations announced that Eve was missing.

The children in her class just could not figure out what had happened. Eddie told his sister that Eve might have hitched a ride on a laser-powered, inter-planetary, asteroid interceptor. Actually, Eddie was kidding just to hide his fear.

Even though he didn't know Eve very well, Eddie was scared for her. In fact, that night while he had his usual trouble falling asleep, Eddie kept tossing and turning and thinking about Eve. He wondered where she could be and whether she was hurt or something. Finally, Eddie did get to sleep. It was very, very late.

Eve Shows Up

After he had been asleep for a while, Eddie suddenly woke up. He said to himself, "I can't sleep anymore. I'm having noisy dreams. I keep hearing something in my head, something banging and knocking and clunking and clapping."

So Eddie sat up in bed. Now he was awake.

But he could still hear those sounds, the knocking and the banging. He thought to himself, "It could be the naughty night knocker who's here to haunt me!"

Eddie looked around. There was a full moon, so he could see out his window. He suddenly noticed a shadow in the window. He quickly threw the covers over his head and rolled up into a ball.

Hot Fudge, who had been lying on the floor, got scared and jumped under the covers with

Eddie. Neither of them wanted to be seen by whatever or whoever was outside the window.

The knocking started again. Eddie decided to be brave. He reached out from under the covers and turned on the lamp. Then he got out of bed. Hot Fudge was not as brave as Eddie—he stayed under the covers.

There in the window, Eddie could now see the face of a girl. It was Eve! It was Eve knocking on Eddie's window. It was not the naughty night knocker, after all.

Eddie opened the window and gasped, "Hey, what are *you* doing here? You're missing!"

Eve, almost crying, answered, "Um . . . not me . . . I'm not missing. I'm starving." Eve spoke slowly. It was always hard for her to think of the right words to say. She added, "I'm sorry. I . . . I shouldn't've bothered you." Eve was really crying now.

Eddie said, "Wait a minute. Wait here. I'll go get you something to eat. Don't disappear. Don't be missing again."

Eddie then went to the kitchen and brought back a glass of milk and some of his favorite peanut butter cookies. He opened the window and handed them to Eve.

"Thanks," said Eve. She was very quiet while she ate the cookies and drank the milk. She still looked upset, but she had stopped crying.

Eddie said, "Now, you'd better go home. Everyone has been worried about you, especially me. You're the nicest kid in the class. I don't want anything bad to happen to you."

Eve didn't say a thing. She was trying to think of something to say, but she always had trouble figuring out how to say things. Finally, she said, "Can I . . . um . . . sleep in your fort . . . the one your father helped you build in your backyard?"

Eddie said, "Okay, okay, but wait a minute." He went to his closet and took out some jeans and a sweater and put them on over his pajamas. Of course, he also put on one of his favorite hats. He grabbed his flashlight and started to crawl out the window. "Let's go," he said. When Hot Fudge heard this, he crawled out from under the blankets, jumped out the window, and followed Eddie and Eve.

Eddie took Eve to the fort. She went inside, sat down, and leaned against the wall. Eddie turned to leave. Then he began to think some more. "What if Eve runs away again?" he thought. "What if she's not here when I come back in the morning? Maybe I should go into the house and call Eve's mom. But then maybe Eve will leave while I'm calling. What do I do?"

Eddie decided he had to stay with Eve so she couldn't run away. So he sat down outside the fort. He planned to take Eve home in the morning when it was light. Eddie tried very hard to stay awake. He made believe he was a guard in the army. But after about an hour, Eddie fell asleep.

The Next Morning

The next morning Eddie's mother went to wake him up. She was shocked to find that his bed was

empty. "Where's Eddie? Where's Eddie?" she shouted.

Becky got up, and so did their father. He said, "Now there are *two* children missing! Something awful is going on around here. I can't even find Hot Fudge. I'd better look around just to be sure before I call the police."

Eddie's father searched all through the house. Then he went out back and looked for Eddie. He even went into the woods behind the house.

Luckily, he heard a familiar sound. It was Hot Fudge snoring. He always snored a lot. Eddie said Hot Fudge could win a snoring contest. The sound was coming from Eddie's fort.

When Eddie's father reached the fort, he found his son and Hot Fudge asleep on the ground outside it.

Eddie suddenly woke up. "What am I doing *here*?" he said. "I can't remember how I got here. I must have turned into a transistorized sleep-walking robot!"

Eddie's father looked angry. Eddie said, "Just kidding, Dad. Don't be mad. I had to guard the fort. Eve's in there. She showed up outside my window last night. She needed a place to stay. I had to keep an eye on her."

Eddie's father stuck his head inside the fort. There was Eve fast asleep on a bench. Eddie's father was so surprised. "Eve! Eve!" he cried. "Am I ever glad to see you! And you, too, Eddie! What a relief!

"Eddie, you should have told us about this during the night. You should have gotten us up. This wasn't very smart of you." Eddie's father looked angry again.

"You two children come with me. Eve, do you know how worried everyone is about you? They think that something bad has happened to you."

As usual, Eve did not say anything. She looked frightened. They all went back to Eddie's house. Eddie's father tried to call Eve's parents. The line was busy, so he drove Eve back home.

Eve's mother could hardly believe her eyes. She was so happy to see her daughter again. She cried as she hugged and kissed Eve.

Barktalk was so happy to see Eve that he could not stop barking. He sounded as if he was singing. Barktalk wanted to make Eve happy, too.

"Eve, Eve, what happened? Where were you?" her mother asked.

Eve Tells Her Story

At first, Eve said nothing. She was so sad. Then she looked up and said, "Mom, I ran away. I had to run away . . . 'cause . . . like . . . um . . . I hate school. I'm so dumb. I can't stand school!" Eve started to cry.

Eve's father hugged her. "Eve, you say that you hate school. We know that school is hard for you. But that's no reason to run away from it.

"Do you know how dangerous it is to run

away? Do you know all the awful things that can happen to a child who runs away? Don't ever think about doing *that* again. Eve, we have a lot to talk about and a lot to think about."

Eve covered her face with her hands. She was so sorry that she had upset her parents by running away. She hated to make anyone unhappy, especially her mother and father.

"Please, Eve," her mother said, "tell us what really happened to you. We need to know. We have to find out the whole story."

Eve knew she had to talk about what had happened, even though she really wanted to forget all about it. It was so hard for her to explain complicated things, and this sure was complicated!

Eve and her parents sat together on the sofa. Eve began talking very slowly. She said, "Yesterday in school I felt . . . like . . . horrible. I wanted to leave . . . to run away . . . far away. I didn't know what to do," Eve sobbed.

"School's so hard; it's too hard. Yesterday was . . . like . . . real hard.

"I couldn't understand Mrs. Grillo. I didn't know what to do on the test. I was afraid Mrs. Grillo would get mad at me for messing up. Mrs. Grillo . . . she's nice . . . I want Mrs. Grillo to like me."

"Mrs. Grillo thinks you're a wonderful child," her mother said.

Eve continued. "I felt bad on the bus," she said. "When I got off, I started to run and run as fast as I could. I didn't know . . . I mean . . . where I was going."

"You must have been so scared," Eve's father said. He put his arm around her shoulder.

"I *was* real scared," Eve agreed.

Eve went on very slowly. "I ran. I just ran, and then I walked. I saw the place with the books . . . uh . . . the library. I went in. I hid where they have all the books. I hid for a long time. I heard someone talking. Then it got dark. It was real, real scary. They turned off all the lights."

"The library must have been closing," her
father said.

"I ran out back. It was dark, too dark to see
much. I didn't know where to go. It was so scary,
so scary." Eve was still upset, but she had stopped
crying.

Eve's parents felt so bad for her. They were
thinking about how Eve must have felt in school
that day.

"Then what happened?" Eve's father asked.

"I went to Eddie's house," Eve answered. "Eddie was nice to me . . . real, real nice. He took care of me till his father found us. Can I go to my room now?"

"Sure you can, Eve," her father said. "Why don't you rest for a while. You must be tired."

Eve went to her room while her parents and sister talked about how to help her.

After a while, Eve came back into the living room. She tried to play the piano, but she didn't really feel like it. Then she started to watch TV, but she didn't like that either. Finally, she just sat and cuddled Barktalk who was glad to have his best friend back again.

Eve didn't say very much for the rest of the day, but she did a lot of thinking. She knew she could think better than she could talk. She thought about how dangerous and scary it was to run away, how something bad could have happened to her. She decided she'd never run away again.

Eve Gets Some Help

On Monday, Eve's parents went to see Mrs. Grillo. They told her that they were very worried about Eve. Eve's father said he thought Eve was **depressed**. He said that she seemed so sad all the time.

Eve's mother said that Eve just didn't seem to feel very good about herself. She said that when Eve was younger, before she ever started school, she was a very happy child. Now she was just plain sad.

Eve's mother also said that Eve used to be interested in so many things. Now she had lost interest in just about everything. She didn't even play with her games or toys. She hardly ever played the piano. She didn't care about anything much except, maybe, her dog Barktalk.

Mrs. Grillo agreed that Eve seemed to be depressed. She was worried about her, too. She said that Eve could see the school psychologist, Dr. Silva, for an **evaluation**.

Dr. Silva would talk to Eve and give her some tests to find out how to help her do better in school. Mrs. Grillo said that a number of children in the class had had evaluations to help them with their learning.

Eve's parents liked Mrs. Grillo's suggestion. They talked to Eve about it. She agreed to take the tests.

When the tests were finished, Dr. Silva told Eve, her parents, and Mrs. Grillo what she had found out.

She said that Eve had real trouble listening in school because she had trouble understanding language. In other words, she had a **language disorder**. That was why she found science so difficult. She also had trouble with all the kinds of mind work you need language for.

Dr. Silva said that Eve had excellent

handwriting. The tests also showed that Eve was very good at remembering things like math facts, punctuation rules, and even spelling words. Eve was much better at remembering than she was at understanding. Often, when she didn't understand something, Eve would just try to remember it.

Dr. Silva agreed with Eve's father that Eve was depressed—she was very, very sad. Dr. Silva said Eve had low **self-esteem**. That meant Eve didn't like herself very much. She believed everyone else was smarter than she was. This included her sister Judy and all the other kids she knew.

Dr. Silva said she would talk with Eve every week to try to help her get over feeling depressed. She also thought Eve would be less depressed if she could do better in school.

Eve Gets More Help

Eve also met with Ms. Goldberg, a **speech and language therapist**. She was a person who helped kids with language problems.

Ms. Goldberg talked to Eve about her problems. She explained that school is full of difficult language. Teachers are always using language to explain things and give directions. Usually, there isn't much time to figure out what the teacher is saying.

"Kids have to use different kinds of language abilities for their mind work in school all the time," Ms. Goldberg said. "Sometimes this is very difficult.

"First of all, kids have to *understand* language. Then, when they are called on in class, they have to think up answers and put these answers into good language very quickly."

Ms. Goldberg said that the language kids have to use in school is harder than the language they use with their friends or at home. In school, they have to keep learning new words, and they have to put together long sentences with the right ideas in them.

Eve took some tests with Ms. Goldberg, too. When they were finished, Ms. Goldberg helped Eve realize why she was having trouble in school.

"You have a problem understanding what you hear and what you read," Ms. Goldberg said. "You are like many kids with language disorders. It's hard to understand what you read when you have trouble understanding what you hear.

"You can figure out letter sounds pretty well. There's another girl in your class who has a lot of trouble with letter sounds. She has a problem reading even single words.

"You can read single words you have never seen before. And you can also read out loud fairly well. But when you see words together in sentences and paragraphs, you have a lot of trouble understanding what they mean.

"Your language disorder also makes it difficult for you to write. And it makes it difficult for you to talk in good sentences so that other people can understand you."

Eve didn't completely understand Ms. Goldberg. But she could tell that she was having trouble with language mind work in school. She learned that her trouble with language did not mean that her whole mind was a problem.

For the first time, Eve realized that there must be a lot of other kids with her kind of mind. Before that, she had thought that she was the only one.

Eve knew how good she was at a lot of things like spelling and music and helping other people. But Eve also knew she needed to work on her language abilities. Ms. Goldberg said she would help her, and Eve was glad.

Eddie Tries to Help Eve

Over the weekend that Eve ran away, Eddie's mother had a talk with him and Becky. She said that Eve had run away because she was so upset about school. She was unhappy because she was having so much trouble understanding her teacher and following directions. Becky and Eddie's mother also talked about how dangerous running away can be.

On the Monday after that weekend, Eddie told all the other kids how he had rescued Eve and how he had kept her in his fort all night. Eddie was a hero. He felt very proud.

Eddie went up to Eve right after school. As they were getting on the bus, he said to her, "Please don't run away today. I need my sleep. I don't want any girly ghouly ghosties knocking at my window.

"And tomorrow in school, if you don't understand something, just ask good old Ever-

Ready-Eddie, or you can even ask Mrs. Grillo. I promise not to laugh at you. I never laugh at you. I can't laugh at you 'cause there's a whole bunch of stuff *I* don't understand, especially when I'm taking a mind trip. A lot of times if you ask questions, *I* can find out what's going on!"

"Thanks, Eddie," said Eve. "I won't run away anymore. It was . . . like . . . so scary. It was the worst thing I ever did. Mom says running away is very, very dangerous. Mom says you should fix a problem. No one should run away from problems."

6. Derek's Kind of Mind

Derek loved science. He was very interested in radios, television sets, and all kinds of electronic gadgets. Derek's father once got him a kit to make a two-way radio. Derek figured out how to put it together without even reading the directions. He spent one whole morning working on it in his bedroom.

As he worked that day, Derek looked out the window and saw a group of kids playing ball across the street. Derek didn't like sports. But part of him wanted to be outside with friends on such a beautiful morning.

When Derek finished building his radio, he called his mother to see if she wanted to try it out, but she was busy with something else. Derek suddenly felt a little sad. How could you talk to yourself on a two-way radio? He had made this great radio, but he had no friends to enjoy it with. Other kids just didn't like Derek.

When it came to schoolwork, though, Derek did very well. He usually got the best marks in Mrs. Grillo's class. He was very good at arithmetic, reading, writing, and spelling. He also knew a whole lot about nature and, of course, science. He told everyone he wanted to be a molecular biologist when he grew up. Other kids didn't even know what that was!

Because Derek was excellent with language, he often used big words when he talked. He seemed to know loads of facts about everything. But Derek had two problems. He had trouble getting along with other kids, and he had a very hard time playing sports.

Derek's Problem with Other Kids

There were many reasons why no one in the class liked Derek. First of all, he was always bragging about how smart he was. Also, he kept making fun of other kids and laughing at their mistakes.

Once, Sonya was trying to read out loud in class. She was having a very hard time. Derek acted as if he was annoyed at her. Finally, he said, "Sonya, you must not be very smart. This book is so unbelievably easy. It's a cinch. Anyone should be able to read it."

Derek said things like that all the time. He didn't know how to be nice. He could hurt someone's feelings or make a kid angry without even realizing it.

Somehow, Derek's mind didn't help him

understand how you need to act and talk in order to get along with other kids. When everyone had to line up for something, Derek would push and shove the other kids. Sometimes he would force his way to the front of the line.

When he was with other kids, Derek often picked the wrong things to talk about. If everyone was acting silly and joking, Derek might suddenly start talking about something very serious and

acting like a grown-up. And if the other kids were talking about something serious, he might interrupt and say something he thought was funny. But usually no one else thought it was funny. Still, Derek would laugh and laugh at what he had said.

Often, when Derek talked, he sounded like a grown-up, not a kid. That bothered the other kids.

One day Mrs. Grillo told the class that they would have to learn twenty new vocabulary words for a test.

Derek raised his hand and said, "But I already know those words, so I'll just use the time to get ahead. I'll learn some more difficult words. I think that learning new definitions will help my mind grow." That didn't sound like a kid talking.

Eddie, who sat near Derek, put his hand on his forehead and cried out, "Oh, no, he talks in nerd's words!"

Kids laughed at the way Derek spoke and at

the things he said. He never understood why they were laughing. But he hated it when they laughed at him.

Bill often whispered bad things about Derek. He told the other kids not to sit near Derek at lunch. Eddie's sister Becky told kids that Derek was yucky, so they shouldn't go near him or they might catch the yuckies. Becky was popular, so the other kids listened to her.

Derek hated being so unpopular. All day, wherever he went, he would hear other kids say, "You can't sit here. This seat is saved." Once in a while, Eve would sit with Derek on the bus or in the cafeteria. She didn't really like him, but she felt sorry for him.

At home after school, Derek usually had to play by himself or with his dog Superstar. Superstar got his name because he could run fast and catch balls in his mouth. And no one could beat Superstar in his very favorite game, tug-of-war.

Superstar loved Derek. He and Derek never insulted each other. But Derek still wanted kids for friends, too. Derek wanted friends so badly that sometimes he would go off where no one could see him (except Superstar) and he would cry. Superstar would cry, too. That's because he got sad whenever he saw Derek sad.

Derek's Problem Playing Sports

Derek had a hard time when he played sports. He just couldn't play as well as the other kids. He had trouble throwing and catching a ball. He was bad at kicking, too. He ran slowly, and he looked funny when he ran. Derek's kind of mind was not so good at getting his muscles to work together smoothly in sports.

Whenever the kids were going to play a game, Derek was always chosen last for a team. No one wanted Derek on their side. That made him sad and angry.

Once, when Bill said that he didn't want
Derek on his team, Derek said to him, "You think
you're so great just because you can play soccer.
What's so special about that?" But Derek had a
secret wish that he could play as well as most
other kids.

A Trip to the Lake

One day in the spring, Mrs. Grillo told the class
that they would be going on a field trip to the

lake. They would study the plants and animals that live in the water and on the shore. The children would be able to study little fish called minnows, and they would find out about snails, crawfish, frogs, and dragonflies.

When Eddie heard about the trip, he became very excited. He jumped up out of his seat, saying, "Oh man, cool, cool, cool! Flying dragons, flying dragons! Super! I'll have to look for the flyin' braggin' draggin' dragon! He's always braggin' about how he can be draggin' other dragons while he's flying."

"Eddie, that's enough of that," Mrs. Grillo warned.

"Okay, okay," Eddie said, "but one more thing. Wouldn't it be great to invent a satellite that looks like a dragonfly or a flying dragon or even a flying wagon—a jet-powered flying dragon wagon!"

Eddie settled down, and Mrs. Grillo told everyone that they would not have to spend the whole day learning about water animals. There would be time to play games. She would bring along a kickball.

When Derek heard about the kickball, he felt worried. Everyone else thought the trip would be great fun. But Derek was not at all happy. He said to Eddie, "Sounds boring to me—very, very boring."

But Eddie was all excited. He thought he might even see some tadpoles. Eddie loved tadpoles. They reminded him of his flying frogship.

The Day of the Trip

The big day arrived. Everyone was excited, everyone except Derek. He didn't want to go. But his mother told him he had to.

Derek thought maybe his father could convince his mother to let him stay home. His parents were divorced, so Derek ran to the phone to call his dad at his apartment across town. But his father agreed with his mother that Derek should go on the trip. He told Derek to bring along his camera so he could photograph different plants and animals.

Derek asked if he could take pictures instead of playing kickball. His mother said she would ask Mrs. Grillo. Derek's mother was one of the parents going on the trip.

Everyone met at the bus outside the school. The kids were all picking somebody to sit with. But Derek was all by himself, as usual. And, as usual, he pretended he didn't care.

Derek never had trouble getting along with children much younger than he was. He also got along with grown-ups. They thought he was so smart. But he just couldn't get along with kids his own age.

As soon as they got to the lake, Mrs. Grillo told everyone to come down to the edge of the water. The children gathered around their teacher.

As usual, Derek pushed away a couple of kids so that he could be right in front.

Mrs. Grillo asked, "What should we expect to find in the water along this shore?"

Derek raised his hand and yelled, "I know! I know! I know! This water contains millions of tiny microscopic, one-celled plants and minuscule animals as well as other organisms of various species."

"What's an organism?" asked Sonya.

Eddie quickly answered, "I think it's some kind of musical instrument that plays under water."

"Oh, no," Derek responded. "It's a living thing."

Eddie then answered, "*You're* a living thing. You're not even a kid. You're just a *thing*, a living *thing*."

Mrs. Grillo told the children that they shouldn't say mean things to each other.

They all walked along the shore. Bill was

making a list of each kind of animal and plant that they saw. It was his job to keep a record. Because Bill had memory and writing problems, Mrs. Grillo repeated some things so that he could write them down.

Derek knew the most about the different plants and animals. And he made sure that everyone realized how much he knew. That made the other kids a little angry and maybe even jealous. Derek didn't seem to understand that he shouldn't brag so much about all he knew.

The Kickball Game

When everyone was finished looking at the plants and animals, it was time to play kickball. Mrs. Grillo went to get the ball. As she was coming back with it, Derek told her that he definitely did not want to play.

Mrs. Grillo said that Derek really should try. She told him he'd never get better at games like

kickball if he didn't practice. But she could see that Derek was starting to cry because he was too embarrassed to join the other kids. He hated to have them see how bad he was at sports.

"Okay, Derek," Mrs. Grillo said. "You don't have to play. But I want you to stay nearby. Don't wander off into the woods or anything like that."

Derek took some pictures of the lake. Then he sat down at the edge of the woods and watched the kickball game.

Once again, Derek was alone. He was used to being by himself, but he still didn't like it. He wished, at least, that his dog Superstar could be with him. "Superstar probably plays kickball better than I do," Derek thought to himself.

As Derek watched the game, it was Eddie's turn to kick the ball. Sonya rolled it towards Eddie. He was supposed to kick it as far as he could and then run to first base.

When the ball arrived, Eddie kicked it with all his might. It went far off into the air. Everyone was amazed to see how far Eddie could kick the ball. He started to run really fast toward first base.

But on the way, Eddie saw a butterfly, a large yellow butterfly.

Eddie shouted, "Look at the yellow-winged, laser, butter-powered asteroid! Look at it go!" Eddie flapped his arms like wings and took off after the butterfly.

Bill, who was on Eddie's team, yelled at him to pay attention. But Eddie continued to chase the butterfly. He never made it to first base.

Bill came over to him looking very angry. He said, "Eddie, why can't you concentrate? Why can't you ever pay attention? You'd be a great player if you weren't so hyper."

Eddie answered, "This is a dumb game, and it's a boring game. Besides, I feel sorry for the ball. How would you like anyone to kick you just for fun?"

Eddie left the game. The butterfly asteroid

landed on a leaf, but Eddie couldn't find it. He went and sat down on the ground next to Derek.

Eddie leaned over and said, "Kickball's a really, really, really dumb game. It's absolutely, completely boring in every boring way. I'd rather take exciting mind trips or play video games in my head any day."

Derek answered, "Yeah, it sure looks boring."

Eddie glanced at Derek and said, "You're smart. That's why you don't play. You're too smart to play. I can't play because I'm too subtractible. I mean I'm too *distractible*."

Derek asked, "What do you mean?"

Eddie said, "I mean I can't think about what I'm doing long enough. Something else pops into my mind, something I see or remember or hear. Then I start thinking about whatever popped into my mind instead of the thing I'm doing."

Derek was quiet. Then he said in a very soft voice, "I don't play because I can't play. I'm too clumsy. I can't run fast. I can't kick the ball adequately."

Eddie agreed. "Yeah," he said, "you're no good at sports. When you try to run, you look like a rolling balloon full of whipped cream and jello." Eddie laughed, but Derek didn't laugh.

Then Eddie realized that he had said something mean. "I'm sorry, Derek," Eddie said. "I shouldn't say mean stuff like that. Besides, you can't help it if you run funny. Sometimes I say mean stuff too fast without thinking."

Derek looked down at the ground sadly.

Eddie quickly added, "It's okay, Derek. Some kids like Bill and Sonya are born to be good at sports. They have super sports minds and sports muscles. You have a super mind for reading. I have a super mind for thinking up super ideas."

Derek still looked unhappy, even though Eddie was saying all those nice things about him. "Still, I'm horrible, horrible, horrible at sports.

I wish I could play like other kids," Derek answered.

Eddie tried to make Derek feel better. "Derek," he said, "Derek, you're not horrible at sports. You're just terrible. But you're only sort of very terrible, not horrible."

"Thanks," said Derek.

Terriball

Eddie slapped Derek on the back. He started laughing, and then he said, "Man, what you need is a chance to play a sport where you can play terribly and be a star. You need to play Terriball, the world's greatest sport for terrible players.

"The more terribly you play Terriball, the better you'll be at Terriball. Kids who play Terriball without being terrible lose the game. They aren't terrible enough to play Terriball."

Derek answered, "Eddie, sometimes you have ideas that are a little bit strange."

Eddie didn't answer Derek. Instead, he started to look around in the woods and came out with three small rocks which he put down on the ground. He then ran back into the woods and came out a few minutes later with a pile of sticks.

Derek was sitting on the ground watching Eddie. "What are you doing?" he asked.

Eddie answered, "I'm getting ready to teach you how to play Terriball. You are so terrible at

playing ball that you may become the greatest and most terrible Terriball player who ever lived."

Derek looked confused.

"You see these three rocks?" Eddie went on. "These are t-e-r-r-i-b-a-l-l-s. They are the balls you use in this game."

Derek said, "Eddie, those are terrible balls. They're not even round. Balls have to be round. Those are terrible balls."

"Of course, sure," Eddie answered. "You have to play Terriball with terrible balls. If the balls weren't terrible, they wouldn't be terriballs, so you couldn't play Terriball."

"Oh," Derek said. "I guess that makes sense."

Eddie then took one of the largest rocks and began to pound a stick into the ground.

When he finished, he looked up and said to Derek, "Okay, Derek, it's time to play Terriball. You see that stick in the ground in front of the tree? When you put a stick in the ground, it's called a stake. Did you ever play a game with a stake before?"

Derek answered, "The only thing I ever do with steak is eat it. And my mom said that you should never play with your food." Derek laughed at his own joke.

Eddie laughed too. "In this game," he said, "the stake—the stick—goes right in front of that big tree. Here's what you have to do."

Derek interrupted, "I know what you have to do. You have to kick the rock and try to hit the stake with it."

"No, no," Eddie answered. "You lose if you hit the stake. In this game, you have to miss as many stakes as you can.

"To play Terriball terribly, you have to have a lot of missed stakes. Every time you hit the stake, it's a mistake. But, you're so bad at kicking you'll be good at making a lot of missed stakes. You will be getting all those good missed stakes, so you won't make mistakes."

"I see, or I think I see. This looks easy. I know how I can miss the stake. I will just kick the rock behind me!"

"No, no, no," Eddie said. "After the rock misses the stake, it has to hit the tree behind the stake. That's a *big* tree.

"Anyone can hit that tree. Derek, even you can hit that tree. But you have to miss the stake *and* hit the tree with the rock. Go ahead, try it."

Derek had so much trouble kicking that he almost missed the rock completely when he tried to kick it. But he did kick the side of the rock, and he did miss the stake, and the rock did hit the tree.

Eddie cheered and told Derek he was a star terrible Terriball player. Then Eddie put another stick into the ground, so on his next kick, Derek had to miss two stakes and hit the tree.

Eddie kept adding one more stake each time. Derek was able to miss seven stakes and hit the

tree with the stone. He and Eddie were having a great time.

Eddie told Derek, "Derek, you missed all those stakes. Congratulations. You are terrific at making missed stakes. But this is getting a little boring.

"It's my turn now. I have to kick. And I can decide whether I want to win by having the most missed stakes or by hitting the most stakes without hitting the tree.

"You see, from now on, whoever kicks makes up the rules and decides whether a missed stake will be a mistake or if a hit stake will be a mistake."

Eddie decided to try and hit as many stakes as he could. So Derek kept putting more stakes into the ground. He also moved around some of the stakes that were already there.

Soon the other kids finished their kickball game. They came over to the edge of the woods to watch Derek and Eddie. They saw how the two boys kept changing the rules of the game to keep it interesting. They could see how much fun Derek and Eddie were having. The two boys never stopped laughing. They tried to make the rules as funny as possible.

Bill said, "That looks excellent. And it looks like fun. Can I play?"

Eddie answered, "Sure, sure, Bill, you can play. But you can't be serious.

"You're too serious when you play sports. Sports are games. Games are supposed to be a lot of fun, and they can't be a lot of fun unless they're a little funny. To play Terriball terribly, you have to keep laughing and fooling around."

Bill answered, "Okay, I'll try."

"But if you try too hard to win instead of just having fun, we'll call you TerriBill the Terriball Terror."

By now, Derek's mother and Mrs. Grillo were watching the children play. They thought it was great to see everyone having such a good time.

Mrs. Grillo said to Derek's mother, "Isn't it

wonderful that these kids are creating their own game? It's much better than just playing the same old games over and over again without thinking up any new ideas."

"I agree," said Derek's mother. "I think it's so nice to see young people use their imagination while they play." She was very pleased to see Derek having such a good time.

She went over to the children and asked if she could help. She said she could be a judge or a coach.

"No, no, no!" Eddie yelled. "Terriball is a game with no grown-ups. There are no coaches, no judges, no nobodies who are grown up.

"Grown-ups would boss us around. They would make up rules we would have to follow all the time. They would forget it's just a game. That would be horrible. I mean Horrorball. Terriball is completely a kids' game, a 100% kids' game. That's why it's so much fun."

Derek's mother laughed. She was really glad

the kids could play by themselves. Everyone kept taking turns playing Terriball.

Bill decided that the game was silly. He went off alone and practiced with his kickball. He said that he was too good at sports to play such a terrible game. He also knew that he would lose because he would have to act funny instead of serious.

The others were all laughing and having a great time. Each one tried to make silly mistakes. Eddie said that you got an extra point if you did something totally silly.

Derek turned out to be the best player. Eddie said that he was the world champion, the most terrible Terriball player who ever lived. Everyone congratulated him. It was the first time Derek had ever been a hero.

Derek started to think about himself and about how much fun it was to fool around with other kids. He had acted silly during the Terriball game, and the other kids loved it.

He didn't brag, and he didn't talk as if he were so much smarter than everyone else. The kids liked him so much better when he didn't boast or act too grown up.

It was a great day for Derek. He did not get into one argument all day long. Usually, he would get angry with somebody and push him around or call him bad names.

At the lake, Derek realized how much fun it could be to try to be nice to other kids and to try to get them to like you.

Derek Gets Help and Starts To Improve

On the trip back to school from the lake, Mrs. Grillo sat next to Derek's mother. They talked quietly about Derek and about how much he wanted to make friends and be liked by other children. But getting along with others just was not easy for him.

Mrs. Grillo explained that Derek seemed to

be having serious problems with his **social skills**. She said that there are a lot of kids who have a learning disorder that makes it hard for them to understand what they need to say and do to get along with other kids. Often, kids like Derek don't even realize what they're doing wrong—what's making other kids dislike them.

When Derek's mother heard Mrs. Grillo talk about social skills problems, she knew right away that her son needed help with his social skills.

Mrs. Grillo also told Derek's mother that he was having a lot of trouble with his **motor coordination**. Motor coordination is the way your mind and body work together so that your muscles do just what you want them to do. Good motor coordination helps you become excellent at a sport or at artwork.

Derek's mother said she thought that Derek wanted to be good at sports, but he felt so sad when he couldn't play as well as the other kids.

Derek's mother and Mrs. Grillo decided that

it was very important for Derek to get some help both at school and at home.

When she got home, Derek's mother called his father. They agreed that they wanted to try to help their son.

That evening Derek and his mother had a long talk. She explained to him all about his trouble with social skills and his problems playing sports. She also told Derek that she was very proud of him and she wanted him to keep on being very interested in science and reading. But she thought he would be happier if he could play more with other children and get along with them better. Derek felt really glad when his mother told him that his parents and his teacher wanted to help him work on his social skills and his motor coordination.

After that, Derek's father would sometimes take Derek and a friend out to do something together. Afterwards, Derek and his dad would talk about how Derek had behaved. They would decide whether Derek had boasted or tried to sound too grown up. They would discuss what Derek had done to make his friend feel good. In other words, they talked about all the different social skills that Derek needed to learn.

In school, Derek met with a few other students and a **social worker**, Mr. Thompson. A social worker is a person who helps kids and their families when they are having trouble in their lives. Mr. Thompson, Derek, and the other kids would talk about making friends and keeping friends and getting other kids to like you.

Mr. Thompson explained that getting along with other people is a kind of mind work. Everyone has to work to make friends and keep friends. He said that some kids have trouble learning to read or do arithmetic. And others have social skills problems that make it hard for them to work and have fun with other kids.

A few times, Mrs. Grillo talked to the whole class about how important it is for kids to get along with each other. She said it is mean for popular kids to pick on someone with poor social skills. She also said it is unfair not to sit near someone just because that person's kind of mind has trouble with social skills.

Derek wanted to work on improving his motor coordination, too. This kind of mind *work* can also be mind *play*. Derek wanted to play soccer like Bill, so Derek's father helped him. They practiced almost every weekend. Derek decided to try to become good at just one sport and to do it as well as he could.

Little by little, other kids stopped disliking Derek. Instead, they tried to help him get along with other students. Derek began getting telephone calls from other kids. They would ask him questions about their homework since he usually knew the answers. He tried not to act too smart, and he was careful not to tease. Sometimes he still made other kids angry because of what he said or did. But he was definitely getting better. By the end of the year, Derek didn't have to sit by himself on the bus. He was really glad he could stop pretending he didn't mind being alone. It was always so hard for him to make believe he didn't care about his problems.

7. The Minds of
All Kinds School

One day a group of kids were eating lunch together at school when a teacher came over to their table and looked at Eddie. "Eddie," he said, "I can hear you from the other side of the room. You'd better settle down."

Eddie hadn't realized he was making so much noise. He almost never realized it when he was talking too loud. "Okay!" he shouted. "I'm sorry. I'll settle down."

Then the teacher said, "And, Eddie, you're not supposed to play with your food. Take that sandwich off your head." Everyone at the table started to laugh.

Eddie's Lunch Launch

Eddie called out, "You don't understand! You don't understand! I'm getting ready to launch my lunch from my lunch launcher. That sandwich isn't on my head; it's on my lunching pad—I mean my launching head. This is going to be the first unmanned or unwomaned lunch launched into outer space.

"Ladies and gentlemen," Eddie announced, "we're about to set off the world's most powerful rocket fuel. It's a fuel invented by that cool fuel finder, Ever-Ready-Eddie. He is the first person ever to use atomic peanut butter and jelly to launch a satellite lunch into space.

"His launched lunch satellite will spy on the

whole world. Pretty soon he'll find out what everyone in the world is having for lunch. Plus, he'll find out who they're having lunch with, who's sitting at their table."

The other kids were used to Eddie. They enjoyed hearing his imagination at work.

Even the teacher smiled. He told Eddie, "I don't want you to cancel your lunch launching, but I would like you to take that sandwich off the top of your head and let it make a smooth landing in your mouth. Why don't you let it spy on your stomach?"

"Cool! What a neat idea—a stomach spy satellite!" answered Eddie. "Thanks a lot. I'll settle down."

The New Computer

Once most of his sandwich had landed in his stomach, Eddie started to talk about his new computer. His parents had just bought it for everyone in the family to use.

Eddie and Becky were supposed to learn how to use the word processor to help them with their writing. Eddie, of course, was more interested in playing computer games. And, as usual, Eddie had some of his own ideas about how to use the new computer.

Eddie said to the other kids at the table, "Hey, we just got this new computer at home, and I can't stop thinking about it. It can store all kinds of words and numbers and facts in its memory."

"When will *I* be able to do that?" Bill wondered, thinking about his memory problems.

Just then, Derek came along with his lunch. "Can I sit with you?" he asked timidly.

Eddie answered, "Yeah, Derek, sit down. But don't start acting smart. I'm telling everybody about our new, super, awesome computer, the world's most fantastic machine mind."

Eddie continued, " My computer can draw pictures, and it can write neatly."

Bill thought, "I wish *I* could write neatly like a computer."

Derek said, "My mom uses a computer at work. She told me it can write and remember, but it can't come up with ideas of its own. A computer can't think up weird ideas the way Eddie does."

Then Derek said, "But, Eddie, I bet your computer can't talk with other computers."

Everyone laughed, everyone except Eddie. He said, "Don't laugh. Computers *can* talk to each other. They know how to talk just right to each other. They have their own computer words. They can even spy on each other."

Eve thought to herself, "I wonder if computers can talk better than *I* can."

Derek asked Eddie if a computer could help someone get along with other people.

Eddie answered, "It could help you make friends, but you'd have to take it with you everywhere. I'd have to invent a friend-maker computer, a special *pal*culator. You'd just type in a kid's name. Then the pocket palculator would tell you how to get him or her to be your best pal."

Sonya was thinking, too. She wished she had a little computer that could tell her how to figure out the sounds of letters, a decoding computer to help her read.

Eddie kept on describing his computer. He said it could even tell you the date and the time.

Then Bill said, "I know one thing your computer can't do. It can't predict the future.

"I'd like a computer that can tell me about my future. Will I be a professional soccer player when I grow up? Will I always have problems with my memory?"

"And I want to know when I'll be able to understand stuff better," said Eve.

The Grownupulator

Eddie then looked up proudly and yelled,
"Oh man, you guys have come to the right place!
Ever-Ready-Eddie is all ready to tell you about
your future. With his amazing computerized
grownupulator, he will tell you what you will be
like when you grow up. Just come to my house
on Saturday morning, and I will use the
grownupulator disk in my computer to find out
about your future.

"Here's how it works: we just have to put
your kind of mind into the computerized
grownupulator. We type all your strengths and
your weaknesses into it. Then, you can find out
what you'll be doing later in school. Or you can
find out what kind of mind work you'll do when
you grow up."

"I'm all mixed up," Eve admitted.

"So am I," Sonya agreed.

"I guess you'll just have to come and see

how it works for yourself," Eddie told them.

Derek said, "This just sounds like another one of your very weird ideas, Eddie."

"No, Derek, it's not *weird*; it's *wired*."

Derek said, "It's you that's wired weird!"

Eddie yelled out, "No, my grownupulator is wired into the future. For this week only, you can be grownupulatorized free of charge. It's just like I told you. All you need to do is tell the grownupulator about your kind of mind.

"Tell it the things your mind is good at and the things your mind has a little trouble with. In other words, tell it your strengths and weaknesses.

"I will store everything you tell me in the memory of the grownupulator. It will then figure out your future, what you can be like as you get older."

Bill looked sad. He thought to himself, "I can't play soccer all my life. And that's the only thing I'm good at. What will I do after soccer? Maybe I'll be a complete loser. I'm afraid to find out what the grownupulator will say about my future. But I guess I'll go anyway."

All the kids agreed to come to Eddie's house on Saturday morning to get grownupulatorized. Becky said that she didn't know anything about the grownupulator. But it sounded like fun.

Later that day, Eddie told his parents that the children would be coming to play with the computer on Saturday. Their father warned Eddie and Becky, "Remember, kids, a computer is not a toy. Our computer is not some kind of plaything. Just be careful not to break it."

Getting Grownupulatorized

On Saturday, all the kids showed up at Eddie and Becky's house. They all brought their dogs along, too. The dogs played outside while the kids went inside to see the new computer.

Derek's dog Superstar found a huge stick and

SONYA'S
STRENGTHS
AMCNZ
GLRC
HQB4
DQGE

SONYA
DEREK
BILL
BECKY
EDDIE

began to play tug-of-war with Napper. Napper lost because he started to yawn with the stick in his mouth.

Chewsy picked up the stick, so Superstar challenged her to a tug-of-war. Unfortunately, Chewsy chewed up the stick into little splinters.

Then Superstar found a new stick and ran over to Barktalk with it. Barktalk couldn't keep the stick in his mouth because he had so much to

say. You can't hold a stick between your teeth and bark at the same time!

That left only Hot Fudge to play with, but none of the other dogs liked to play with him. Other dogs picked on Hot Fudge. They acted as if he were some kind of dog-wimp.

They would chase Hot Fudge and sometimes even attack him. No wonder Hot Fudge was afraid of other dogs. In fact, while the other dogs played that day, Hot Fudge hid in Eddie's fort.

Meanwhile, Eddie was all excited about showing off the computer. But he hoped the kids had forgotten all about his promise to grownupulatorize them. He didn't really know how he would do that. He was always better at thinking up great ideas than he was at making them work.

Of course, as soon as the other kids arrived, they wanted to find out about their futures. Eddie decided he would have to do some pretending. He would have to pretend to make his computer figure out the futures of the kids. That wasn't very honest, but probably the kids would know he was just fooling around anyway.

Sonya's Future

Eddie said, "Okay, everyone. I'll grownupulatorize each of you, one at a time. It's your turn first, Sonya. Tell me about your mind's strengths and its weaknesses. I will enter them on my gloppy, sloppy disk."

"Well, let's see," Sonya answered. "I'm good at making friends and playing sports. I'm an okay artist. I'm also okay at arithmetic. My mom says I have real good **spatial skills**. That means I'm real good at understanding things through my eyes and knowing how things fit together. I can fix bicycles and eyeglasses. I can make a model without reading the directions."

Eddie interrupted, "Sonya, you sound *too*

good. So far your kind of mind doesn't have *any* weaknesses."

Sonya stopped and wondered whether she should say anything else. It was so hard for her to talk about her mind's weaknesses.

Then she said to herself, "I guess everyone has trouble talking about their weaknesses." So Sonya said out loud, "I just can't read. Reading is the kind of mind work that's hard for me. I'm getting better. But still I have trouble remembering the sounds that letters make."

Eddie started typing away on his computer. He looked up and said, "Okay, I have put Sonya's skill for making things and fixing things into the computerized grownupulator. I have also put in her reading problem. Of course, I have used the secret grownupulator code.

"As you can see on the screen, the grownupulator is starting to tell us something about Sonya."

Becky looked over at the screen. "Eddie, it says, 'Can't find file.'"

"Quiet, Becky," replied Eddie. "You don't understand how this computer works. Everything's in a top secret code."

Sonya said, "That's what reading is like for me, a top secret code that I can't figure out."

"Wait a minute, Sonya," replied Eddie. "The grownupulator has found lots of possibilities for you when you grow up. You could become the best fixer-upper of eyeglasses and bicycles. With your art mind and your math mind, you could design candy-bar wrappers or cereal boxes or even the stuff people wear—like socks."

"I don't want to be a sock designer," Sonya interrupted. "I want to be a teacher. But I could never be a teacher. I can't read. I'm no good with words. Teachers have to read."

"Oh, but Sonya, you *will* read," said Eddie. "Don't give up. My doctor told me everyone can learn. It just takes some kids longer than others.

Look at me. It's taking me a long, long time to
learn how to pay attention and stop some of my
mind trips."

Sonya said, "Yeah, Eddie. My learning
disabilities teacher told me there are lots of very
famous people who couldn't read when they were
kids. They kept trying, and then little by little
they could read. Maybe I *can* be a teacher."

"Okay, Sonya. You're in good shape. We'll
store your strengths in the grownupulator. My

dad says as you get older you get more skills. So you can put in your new skills later. Then the computer will be able to list even more possibilities for your future. Now let's grownupulatorize Derek."

Derek's Future

"There's one thing I know," Derek said. "I know I can't be a football or basketball star. Your grownupulator can't tell me I'll be good at sports."

Eddie looked puzzled. "Derek," he said, "you have just hurt the feelings of my grownupulator. And my mom says that a computer is full of bytes. You'd better not make my grownupulator angry or it might bite you with its million, trillion, zillion bytes!

"And my dad says our computer has lots of hertz in it. I don't know what that means. But I guess if you get computer bytes, it hurts.

"Anyway, Derek, you know you can play sports a little. Look at how good—I mean *bad*—you were at Terriball. It may take you a long time to play other sports well. It's the same with Sonya. It could take her a long time to read well. Someday we may be able to put some sports abilities into the grownupulator for you."

Then Eddie started typing on his computer again. Becky said, "What you're typing makes no sense. It's just a bunch of letters."

"No," responded Eddie. "It's part of my grownupulatorized secret code. Derek will be able to do so many things. He is so excellent at paying attention. He can read well. He knows the world's longest words. He can spell, and he can do math.

"He just can't play sports too much. Derek can make gobs of money. He can invent things. He can be a scientist. He can be almost anything he wants to be.

"But first he has to fix up his social skills, or he'll have to work all alone. He definitely

shouldn't be a cook, though, because he'd gain too much weight."

"Too bad," Derek answered. "I always wanted to work in an ice cream factory."

Bill's Future

"Well," Eddie said, "now it's time to grownupulatorize someone else. Bill, tell us about *your* strengths and weaknesses."

Bill started to answer. "I'm only good at soccer. My muscles are smart. But my mind can't store up things. I'll never be able to do memory mind work when I grow up."

"That's a very, very huge problem," said Eddie. "Poor Bill. What will he do when he's too old for soccer?"

Derek said, "It's okay. I'll give him a job. He can work for me when he's done playing soccer."

Sonya laughed and said, "Nobody would want to work for you. You'd be a mean boss. You wouldn't be nice to people."

Becky interrupted Sonya. "Derek is starting to make friends. Let's give him a chance. Let's see if he keeps getting nicer and nicer."

"Yeah, you're right. I'm sorry," Sonya said.

Bill went on, "Look, guys, I'm no dummy. I had tests, and they found out I'm very good at thinking and understanding. I just have trouble remembering.

"I have trouble remembering math, spelling,

and other school things. My mind can't remember a lot of things even when I understand them."

Eddie said, "We know, Bill. Your mind leaks. Your kind of mind would be super great if it would only stop leaking. Then you could remember facts and skills when you take a test."

"That's me," Bill said. "I'm the kid with the big drain in my brain."

Eddie laughed. "Yup, and that's a huge problem because kids have to remember more than grown-ups. When you're a kid, every day you have to learn tons of new stuff.

"When you're all grown up, there are not that many new things to remember. When I visit my mom in her office, she's always looking stuff up in books or on her computer. She doesn't have to remember as much as we do. Your memory doesn't have to be so fantastic when you grow up."

Bill smiled. "I never thought of that," he said.

Eddie added, "Ever-Ready-Eddie is right. Besides, your memory will get better and better if you keep using it. You can also do tricks to fix your memory leaks.

"Now, as for your future, let's see. You like cars and bicycles. You're awesome at fixing things, too. When you're a grown-up, you can fix cars and jet planes and missiles and satellites."

Bill commented, "Cool, cool, cool. And I'm into motors and engines. I'm really into that stuff."

Eddie said, "You'll be so good at fixing cars that you will have your own car repair shop. Then you'll own two car repair shops and then ten and then twenty car repair shops.

"Pretty soon you'll start building cars. You'll build supersonic, computerized, collapsible, mountain-climbing, solar-powered submarine cars.

"You might even invent cars that you can play soccer in. They'd be called soc-cars. They

would have legs instead of wheels. People would go to soc-car games and soc-car races."

Derek then said, "Bill's cars will be able to go under water like tadpoles and also jump over trees. They will be fueled by atomic peanut butter and jelly."

Everyone laughed, and Eddie said, "That sounds like something *I* would say."

Becky said, "See, Derek, you're making

everyone laugh. Your social skills are better already."

"Someday I'll buy my own red and gold Billmobile," Eddie said. "But now it's time to grownupulatorize Eve. Eve, tell us about your strengths and weaknesses."

Eve's Future

Eve said, "I love animals. I like music. I'm good at helping people. I want to help people, people who are unhappy, people who are sad.

"I can read out loud okay. I have some trouble understanding. I have big problems understanding my teacher. I hate talking in class. Ideas sound dumb when I say them. I'm shy too."

Eddie typed away at his grownupulator. "This is a tough one," he said. "It says here that you will have a job teaching sad animals how to play the piano. You will be the world's first music teacher for unhappy animals. You'll be real famous, and you'll have excellent students—mostly goldfish and gerbils."

Derek asked, "Can she teach my guinea pig to play the violin?"

Sonya added, "Yes, and I want my gerbil to sing."

"No problem, no problem," said Eddie. "She'll even teach Hot Fudge to play the trumpet."

Eve then looked sad and said, "What if I don't want to be a music teacher for animals?"

Eddie responded, "Why wouldn't anyone want to give guitar lessons to pet hermit crabs? They could crawl back and forth on the strings. That would be awesome.

"But there are other kinds of mind work that you can do. That's what's so good about being a grown-up. My dad says grown-ups can have so many different kinds of fun. And there are millions of kinds of jobs that they can do.

"He says when you're a kid, everyone has to go to school. Everyone has to study the same subjects all day. When you're big, you can do the kinds of mind work you like to do, the jobs you're good at. You can get better and better at what you're already good at. You don't get to play as much, but your job can be like playing.

"Eve, you can be a musician or a mental doctor who helps people with their problems or a veterinarian—you know, a doctor for animals. But first you'll have to get better at talking and at

understanding. If you're all mixed up all the time, you'll have trouble with any job."

Eve said, "I know that. But now I know I have a language problem, so I can work on it . . . you know . . . like to get better, to get good at words and sentences and stuff like that."

Becky's Future

Eddie then announced, "Now for the moment we've all been waiting for. It's time to grownupulatorize my sister Becky."

Becky spoke up. "Forget it. This is silly. I don't want to know my future. I want to be surprised when it comes."

"Okay, okay, Becky," Eddie answered.

Eddie's Own Future

Then Eddie asked everyone, "Now you know about my grownupulator. Isn't it great?"

Derek answered, "I think your grownupulator is colossal—it's utterly extraordinary."

"Where do you get words like *utterly*?" Eddie asked. "Your mind's computer must have a nerd processor in it!"

Sonya interrupted, "Eddie, you forgot to grownupulatorize yourself. How about *your* future? What about *your* strengths and weaknesses?"

"Hmm . . . ," began Eddie, "I was hoping you wouldn't ask."

Derek said, "Eddie, you need to be honest, like the rest of us."

"Well," said Eddie, "I have an attention deficit."

"What? What in the world is an invention deficit?" asked Sonya.

"Sonya, you're having trouble with word sounds again," said Eddie. "It's not an *invention deficit*. It's an *attention deficit*. I'm excellent at inventing, but I am not so good at paying attention.

"You know how Bill's mind leaks? Well, my mind takes trips. It travels far out into outer space, way off into dream worlds. Most kids dream mostly while they're asleep. But I have dreams all day long, too. I can only pay attention when stuff is very, very exciting.

"I can concentrate on playing video games and riding my skateboard. I can think about rockets or watch TV for hours and hours and hours.

"But my mind tunes out in class. I look around. I stare out the window. I wonder about what I'm going to do on Saturday. I listen to sounds in the hall. I think about Big Frank's Big Franks, about my dog Hot Fudge, about the super presents I want for my birthday. When I try to pay attention in school, I get bored and my mind feels tired."

Eve said, "I know how you feel, Eddie. The same thing happens to me sometimes. When I don't understand things, I have trouble paying attention, and then I start feeling tired and bored in school."

Then Eddie said, "My doctor said everyone has trouble with attention sometimes. But me, I have trouble with attention too much of the time. That's because of my attention deficit.

"I was born with my attention deficit. My doctor said loads of kids are born with mind problems. Bill was born with his leaky mind. And Derek was born with sports problems and problems getting along with other kids. And Eve was born with problems talking right and understanding language. And Sonya was born with a reading problem. Probably everyone's got some sort of problem. No one's perfect."

Becky nodded her head. "Some kids think I'm lucky just 'cause I'm good at sports and 'cause I have a lot of friends and 'cause I do okay in school."

Eddie interrupted, "I think you're the grossest witch-monster that ever lived. You think you're great. You try to be too perfect. But you're boring, boring. I'm going to invent a computer that has a special trans-sister in it. When you plug it in, your sister gets transferred to another room so she can't keep bugging you."

Bill said, "Cool it, cool it, you guys. How come brothers and sisters fight so much?"

Becky said, "Don't listen to Eddie. My brother's a brat. I'm not perfect. I have problems, too. Sonya knows 'cause she's my very best friend. She knows that sometimes I wet my bed. Eddie knows that, too. He keeps telling me I smell yucky in the morning when I wet my bed at night."

Eddie nodded his head. "Man, you do!"

Eddie then spoke up again. "So my sister wets her bed sometimes, and I have an attention deficit. So what? No one's perfect. There's no such thing as a perfect anybody. A completely perfect kid would be completely, perfectly weird.

"Besides, probably we all feel really bad about ourselves sometimes. That's okay. My doctor says a little worrying is good practice while you're a kid. He says when we worry about ourselves, we learn how to think about our problems better."

Derek thought, "That's right. I go to a social worker for my problems. He told me that you have to think about your problems and work on them. If you make believe you have no problems when you're a kid, then you'll be in real trouble when you grow up and have to solve bigger problems."

A Really Cool School

Eddie jumped out of his seat. "Okay, ladies and gentlemen. Enough of this problem talk. The great moment has come! The grownupulator is ready to tell you all about the great future of the great Ever-Ready-Eddie.

"You know your friend Eddie, the Eddie who makes you laugh, the Eddie who does everything much, much too fast without thinking? Well, this same old Ever-Ready-Eddie will become the world-famous *Mr.* Ever-Ready-Eddie because he will someday start the best school in the whole, entire world!

"It will be the most super, excellent school where everyone will find a way to be excellent and to feel excellent. We'll call it *The Minds of All Kinds School*. It will be a school where every boy finds out all about his mind, and every girl finds out all about her mind. Kids will even learn about each others' minds! It will be a school where all kids feel great about their kinds of minds.

"It will also be a no-cruel school. No one will make fun of anyone else. No one will ever feel embarrassed. All the kids will feel proud of the different kinds of minds they have. Different kids will be allowed to learn in different ways and to do things in different ways."

"That would be completely awesome," said Sonya.

"Our school will be awfully awesome," Eddie agreed. "On the outside, the school will look like the world's hugest fort. The lights and heating will be run on rain power, sun power, and wind power.

"Kids will have to work hard to get excellent at the things they're good at. Everyone in the school will become an expert at something.

"Kids like Bill will have to become superstars at cars and engines. Then, if they want to, they can become the world's greatest car builders and car fixer-uppers.

"Kids like Eve will get to be better and better at playing the piano and learning how to help people with problems. Everybody will know more than anybody else about something."

Bill then looked up and said, "My special teacher said that when you learn a whole lot about something, it can help your memory get stronger. If you can remember a lot about the

things you're an expert in, then maybe you can start remembering other things better, too."

Eddie said, "Right on. Super. If a kid learns all he can about cars, then he'll remember all about cars. His memory will get good exercise. It will get stronger and stronger, and it won't leak as much. Then, maybe he'll remember other important things in school."

Derek said, "If I went to that school, I'd be the leading expert on lizards. I just love lizards. I want to know more about them. I wish I could spend five years learning more and more about lizards. I'd know more about the lives of lizards than anyone else in town."

Eddie said, "Derek, you'd be the lizard-wizard. And you'd still be a little nerdy. But that would be okay, too—as long as you're not cruel to anyone. These are excellent, cool, fantastic ideas. This will be the greatest school on earth. Soon all schools will try to be Minds of All Kinds Schools.

"The teachers will know all about all kinds of minds. They will know the best way for everyone to learn. They will help kids learn more about how learning works.

"Teachers will explain all about memory and teach kids tricks to remember stuff like multiplication tables, spelling words, and new vocabulary.

"Kids will be able to do things in teams. When you grow up, you have to work in teams. Some kids will take tests and write reports together.

"A kid like Eve could use her good handwriting to help someone like Bill. Bill's handwriting is gross. He could tell Eve his good ideas, and she could write them down for him.

"A girl like Eve could also help a boy like Bill remember stuff like punctuation and capitalization.

"Someone like Bill could help someone like me—a kid with an attention deficit. Bill could help a kid slow down and think more before doing something.

"He could remind someone who is having a mind trip to tune back in to the teacher. Kids would all help each other."

Becky said, "That sounds cool. Everybody wouldn't be trying to be the same. Kids would all be glad they have different kinds of minds. They'd all be glad that they are excellent at different kinds of mind work."

"I can tell you now," Eddie said, "I'll need my sister Becky to make real big decisions, to make sure things run smoothly, and to handle all the little details. So Becky will be the principal.

"Bill, you and Derek will coach the Minds of All Kinds Terriball Team. You'll do this when you can get away from the automobile repair shop you'll be the boss of. Wait! I forgot. Terriball has no coaches. Bill, you'll have to be the soccer coach.

"Derek, you should be the kindergarten

teacher because little kids like you so much. And you may be better at sports than those five-year-old kids!

"Eve, you can be the guidance counselor. You'll help kids who are having problems. You should be able to give kids a lot of good advice.

"Sonya, you're so good at art—I'll make you the boss of the Art Department. You can also fix broken eyeglasses and bicycles."

Sonya said, "That sounds great. I would love to be an art teacher. But Eddie, what are *you* going to do?"

Eddie answered, "I'm going to be the boss of brainstorming."

Bill asked, "What's brainstorming?"

Eddie answered, "Brainstorming is when you let your mind take trips and have great new ideas. These ideas make you think about other ideas and then even more ideas. You brainstorm to solve problems, to make new inventions, or to think up great stories.

"Every kid in The Minds of All Kinds School will become a star brainstormer in some way. All kids will have to do brainstorming projects about things they're interested in. Every kid will do a brainstorming project every year.

"And I will be the boss of the brainstorms. I will help kids set off lightning and thunder and snow and rain in their heads so their brains will have exciting storms."

Eve said, "That sounds neat!"

Then Eddie got up and left the room, but the other kids kept on talking.

Becky said, "Let's make sure our school has lots of vacations and recess. It should be a school for dogs and cats, too. The cats can learn to be great tree climbers. The dogs can work at being the best hole diggers and bone chewers."

Sonya laughed as she said, "You're starting to sound just like your brother Eddie."

"Where *is* Eddie?" Eve asked.

Everyone called, "Eddie! Eddie!" but there

was no answer. They all went outside and looked for Eddie, but he was nowhere in sight.

Then they remembered where Eddie went most of the time when he disappeared—his fort. So that's where they went, and, of course, they found Eddie. He had a board on his lap and was drawing *Minds of All Kinds School* on the board.

Eddie said, "School will never be boring with all kinds of minds doing all kinds of special mind work and exciting mind play. Soon every school will want to have all kinds of minds in it. Then the whole world will be kind to every kind of mind."

The kids were so busy talking that they didn't notice their dogs running around barking and playing and having a great time. The dogs were all so different.

One of them was Hot Fudge. He had come out of his hiding place in the fort. Hot Fudge was not as tough as the other dogs. He was making wimpy squeaks as he always did.

Usually none of the other dogs wanted to play with Hot Fudge. Most of the time they just chased him away. But this time, the other dogs had stopped and were watching Hot Fudge. He was digging a hole in the hard soil.

Hot Fudge made a deep, deep hole in less than a minute. He pulled out a huge bone that had been buried in the ground. Boy, was he proud! He had smelled that bone deep in the earth.

Maybe Hot Fudge's sports skills weren't good enough for him to keep up with the other dogs. But his kind of dog mind was excellent at telling paw nails and leg muscles what to do, so he had terrific fine-digging skills. And with his awesome dog memory, he could easily remember all of his smelling rules! For the first time, the other dogs were very impressed with Hot Fudge.

8. Time to Remind Your Mind

So far, in *All Kinds of Minds* we have learned about Eddie and his friends. We found out that each of them had a different kind of mind and that each kind of mind was good at doing different kinds of mind work. But we also saw that each of these children had a learning disorder that made doing certain things in school very hard. Their learning disorders were not their fault and their learning disorders did not mean that these students were dumb or stupid.

All Kinds of Minds has taught us that there are different kinds of learning disorders. We learned about some of them in this book.

- Eddie had an attention deficit.
- Sonya had a reading disorder.
- Bill had memory problems.
- Eve had a language disorder.
- Derek had both social skills problems and motor skills problems.

This chapter will review these six kinds of learning disorders. It will also give you some more ideas about kids who have learning disorders and what can be done to help them do better with different kinds of mind work.

More about Attention Deficits

As we know, Eddie had an attention deficit. There are many boys and girls who have problems with attention. Sometimes these kids are said to have ADD or ADHD, which are other names for attention deficits.

What You Should Know about Kids with Attention Deficits

1. Kids with attention deficits find it hard to concentrate. This means their minds keep "tuning in" and "tuning out." When they tune out, these kids pay attention to things that are not important at the moment. This makes them miss important things.

2. During class, they may take "mind trips" (as Eddie did), stare out the window, listen to a clock ticking, or think about something they saw on television the night before.

3. Sometimes their minds feel too tired or

bored in school. This happens especially when they are supposed to be sitting and listening or trying to do their school work.

4. Kids with attention deficits often have minds that go too fast. So they may make a lot of careless mistakes.

5. Sometimes their bodies move too much. When that happens, people say they are **hyperactive**. They fidget or walk around when they should settle down. This keeps them from getting their work done and bothers people around them.

6. A lot of times, kids with attention deficits do or say things without thinking enough first. So, they are **impulsive**. This means they do or say things they didn't mean to do or say. Sometimes this gets them into trouble.

7. Some children with attention deficits seem to want new games or toys or excitement all the time. When they want something, they want it *too* badly.

Many children with attention deficits are very smart in interesting ways. They have great ideas that other kids or grown-ups would never think of. They can do a lot of things well when they are young and when they grow up. Of course, they can do especially well when they try to make their attention stronger. The diagram on page 236 shows what happens when attention is working well.

What Happens When Your Attention Is Working Well

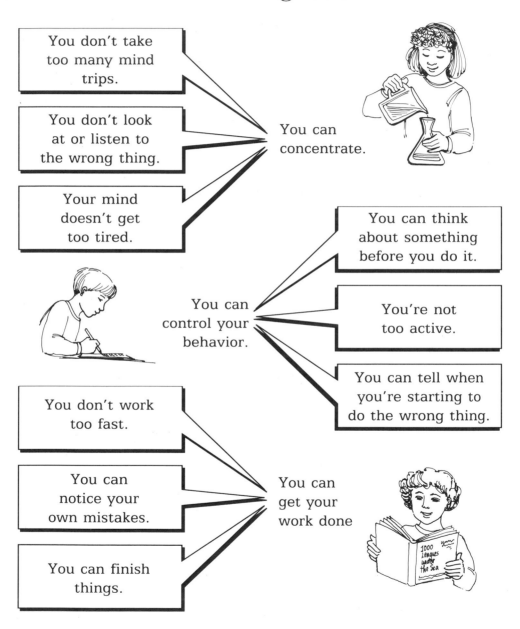

You don't take too many mind trips.

You don't look at or listen to the wrong thing.

Your mind doesn't get too tired.

You can concentrate.

You can think about something before you do it.

You're not too active.

You can tell when you're starting to do the wrong thing.

You can control your behavior.

You don't work too fast.

You can notice your own mistakes.

You can finish things.

You can get your work done

How Kids with Attention Deficits Can Help Themselves

Children with attention deficits should try to know when they are not concentrating well. Eddie learned to tell when he was about to have a mind trip in school. Then he was able to stop it. Any kid can say to himself or herself, "Oops, I'm daydreaming. I'd better tune back in and hear what the teacher is saying."

Children with attention deficits should try to sit close to the teacher. Sometimes the teacher may need to give a little signal when the student is tuning out or having a mind trip. That's what Mrs. Grillo did with Eddie.

A lot of times, kids with attention deficits need to *slow down*. They should tell

---

* You will notice that sometimes pictures of geese are used instead of numbers in this book. Why geese? The geese are used because Dr. Levine raises geese on his farm. He thinks they are very interesting and a lot of fun. They, too, have all kinds of minds and do all kinds of mind work. Geese are often used as artwork in Dr. Levine's books.

themselves to stop and think *before* they do things. Then they won't be so impulsive.

Before doing anything important, they should ask themselves: "What's the best way to do this? What will happen if I do it *this* way? What will happen if I do it *that* way?" Planning like this makes mind work turn out a lot better.

Planning can also help kids behave better and make friends more easily. Before saying something, a kid should wonder: "How will he feel if I say this?" And before doing something, a kid should think: "Will she like me if I do this?"

Kids with attention deficits need to work on watching what they are doing *while* they are doing it. Then they won't make so many careless mistakes in their work.

They have to work very hard to concentrate on their homework. They should find a good place to work. Some kids may need to work in several places. They can do a little bit of work in one room. Then, they can do some more work in another room. They can do some on the floor and then some at a table or desk. Changing locations helps them rewind their minds.

They should pick a good time to do their work. They should take a lot of breaks. They may need to keep getting up and walking around.

They should try writing while they are reading. They can put lines under important words in a book. They can write important words on pieces of paper that stick to the page. Using a pencil in these ways helps a kid concentrate.

They should try to have a grown-up to talk to about their attention deficits. Someone needs to help them keep track of how their attention is doing in school.

Medicines are sometimes used to help kids concentrate better. They help kids slow down, tune in better, and plan more. Ritalin, Dexedrine, and Cylert are three of the pills that are sometimes used. The pills do not make anyone smarter, and they don't completely fix attention problems. But sometimes they help a lot.

More about Reading Disorders

Sonya had a reading disorder. This is a very common kind of learning disorder. It is sometimes called **dyslexia**. Sonya had a hard time reading words. She couldn't figure out the sounds the letters make. Sonya's trouble with reading made her unhappy in school.

Some Important Things to Know about Students with Reading Disorders

1. They usually take a long time to learn the sounds that letters and words make. This is called a **decoding** problem. That's because learning to read is like learning to figure out a secret code.

2. As many children with decoding problems get better, they can remember how to read more and more words. But some children keep on having trouble figuring out the sounds in *new* words and *long* words.

3. When children have a hard time reading words, they often have trouble understanding what they read. This is called a **reading comprehension** problem. Many children who start out with a decoding problem end up with a reading comprehension problem.

4. Sometimes, if kids have trouble reading, they don't want to read at all. They hate to

read. Maybe that's because reading is embarrassing to them or just too much mind work.

Reading is pretty complicated. To read well, you have to do a lot of different things. These different things are shown on the chart on page 243.

Help for Kids with Reading Disorders

 Kids with reading disorders need to get help from a tutor or learning disabilities teacher like Mr. Nasser, who helped Sonya. They get this help with a few other kids or sometimes by themselves. The learning disabilities teacher tries to find the best way to teach each student how to figure out words and how to understand what he or she reads.

Reading

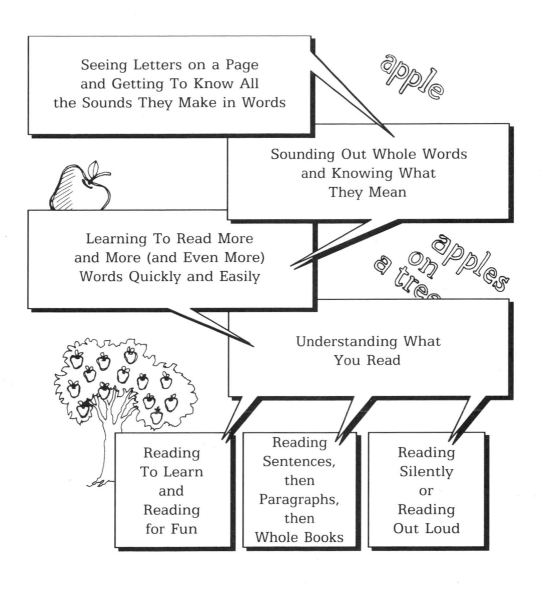

Seeing Letters on a Page and Getting To Know All the Sounds They Make in Words

apple

Sounding Out Whole Words and Knowing What They Mean

Learning To Read More and More (and Even More) Words Quickly and Easily

apples on a tree

Understanding What You Read

Reading To Learn and Reading for Fun

Reading Sentences, then Paragraphs, then Whole Books

Reading Silently or Reading Out Loud

Children with decoding problems should get lots of practice.

- They can do special practice called **drill**. For this, they can use flash cards to practice reading groups of letters and words faster and faster.

- They can play special reading games that will help them remember the sounds that go with letters. Sometimes they can play these games on a computer like Eddie's.

- They can learn about groups of words that go together. For example, they can learn many of the words that end in *ight*. These are called **word families**.

- They can read books with lots of pictures in them. The pictures give good clues about the words.

- They can read about subjects they like and things they know a lot about.

- They can read all kinds of things—books, magazines, newspapers, comics, signs on the road, and even cereal boxes!
- They can take turns reading with an adult—like their mother or father.
- They can read along when someone reads to them. Or they can read along with tapes. They can even do that with this book!
- They can do a whole lot of silent reading.
- Most of all, they can keep on reading. They *have* to if they are going to build up their reading skill.

The easier it is to read, the more fun it is. This means that the mind work needed for reading can be fun, too—especially if you read about subjects you think are interesting. Still, fixing up a reading problem can take a long time. Some kids get discouraged when their reading doesn't get better as fast as they'd like it to. But as long as they don't give up, they can learn to read sooner or later.

More about Memory Problems

Memory is like a dresser or a desk with lots of drawers in it. You put things like facts, ideas, and skills into your "memory drawers" where you keep them until you need to use them.

Memory work is a very important kind of mind work in all school subjects. You can see many of the things we need memory for on page 247.

Memory Mind Work

To do the right things in school, you need

- to remember what the teacher says when she explains something or gives directions.
- to remember the rules—all the things you're supposed to do and all the things you're not supposed to do.
- to remember assignments—like your homework.
- to remember what to take home and what to bring to school.

To read well, you need

- to remember which sounds go with which letters.
- to remember what different words mean.
- to remember important things you've read.

To write well, you need

- to remember quickly how to form letters.
- to remember rules—like how to punctuate and when to capitalize.
- to remember spelling.
- to remember the facts and what you meant to say.
- to remember words—vocabulary—to get your ideas on paper.

To be good at arithmetic, you need

- to remember facts—like $2 \times 3 = 6$.
- to remember sequences—the order of things—like the order of steps to follow to carry numbers when you add.
- to remember the meanings of arithmetic words—like *multiplication*.

If *your* memory is working well right now, you can remember how much trouble Bill had with his memory in school.

Some Things to Remember about Kids with Memory Problems

1. There are different kinds of memory problems.
   - Some children just can't seem to remember *new* skills (like how to do cursive writing) or *new* facts (like the multiplication tables) even right after they have just finished studying them.
   - Some students are able to remember new skills or facts for a short while, but then they forget them. So, a kid may know her new spelling words before she goes to bed, but the next day she will have forgotten them.
2. There are kids who have trouble remembering certain *kinds* of things.
   - It's hard for some kids to remember things they see.

- Other kids have trouble with things they hear.

- Some kids have trouble remembering exact facts—like the capitals of countries.

- Other kids have trouble remembering how to do certain things—like long division.

- Many kids have trouble remembering things in the right order—like the months of the year.

- A lot of times, a kid has more than one kind of memory problem. (Bill had trouble remembering facts *and* sequences.)

3. Children with memory problems often have a very hard time with writing. While you write, you have to remember so many different things all at once. You need to remember spelling, punctuation, vocabulary, capitalization, ideas, facts, and how to make letters. You also have to remember what you meant to write about when you started.

4. Sometimes students with memory problems also have other kinds of learning disorders.

They may have trouble with attention *and* memory. Some have both memory problems *and* language disorders. And, there are kids who have a hard time with memory *and* language *and* their attention.

5. Sometimes students with memory problems work too slowly. This is because it takes them too long to remember their facts or how to do certain things.

Kids with memory problems often feel sad about school. Because remembering is so hard for them, they may think their minds are just not meant for school work. They may feel dumb, but they're not. They just have trouble storing and finding things in their minds' memory drawers!

Help for Kids with Memory Problems

 Kids with memory problems can use a lot of memory **strategies**. These are little tricks that make it easier to remember things.

- They can whisper to themselves. They can repeat what they want to remember over and over.

- They can draw pictures or charts of what they are trying to remember.

- They can make up little games to test themselves to make sure they are remembering what they are studying.

 There are many other things that can make a memory problem less of a problem.

- Students who have trouble remembering math facts can use a calculator.

- A tape recorder can help a kid remember her ideas. She can record her ideas for a story before she writes the story. That way she won't forget what she was going to write about.

- Students with memory problems can be given more time to finish their work and take tests.
- They can be given shorter tests.
- They can spend more time on their homework than other kids do.

Sometimes it is hard for kids with memory problems to think and write at the same time. This is because the memory part of writing is so hard. They can write in steps.

- First, they can think up good ideas.
- Then, they can jot down these ideas.
- After that, they can write without worrying about things like spelling and punctuation.
- Finally, they can rewrite and fix up things like spelling and punctuation.

Memory mind work is easier if you don't do too many things at one time. If you have a memory problem, always try to do things— like writing—in steps.

More about Language Disorders

Eve had a language disorder. She had real problems with words and sentences. This sometimes made it very hard for Eve to understand her teacher. Her language disorder also made it hard for Eve to read and write well. Sometimes she had trouble talking easily when she was with other kids. Many children have language disorders like Eve's.

School is filled with language mind work. Some of the different language abilities you need in school are shown on page 254.

Language Abilities

Understanding Language

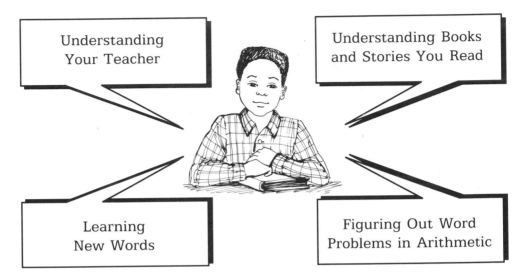

Understanding Your Teacher

Understanding Books and Stories You Read

Learning New Words

Figuring Out Word Problems in Arithmetic

Using Language

Explaining Things

Answering Questions

Writing Down Your Own Ideas

Telling Stories or Talking about Something You Did

You need good language skills for reading and for solving word problems and learning new words (like *denominator*) in arithmetic. Language is important for understanding a teacher when she or he explains something or asks you to do something. You also need language skills so you can explain or describe things to other people. It's not surprising that kids with language disorders can have trouble with a lot of different subjects.

Some Important Things to Know about Students Who Have Language Disorders

1. They often have trouble *understanding* language as well as everyone else. Or it may be hard for them to *use* language for talking and for writing. There are also some students (like Eve) who have trouble *both* with understanding *and* with getting their ideas into language.

2. Students who cannot say their ideas easily may become very quiet and shy in school.

It's just too hard for them to figure out how to say what they need to say. They also have trouble saying it fast enough. Sometimes they are afraid that what they want to say will come out wrong. Then they think they'll sound weird or dumb.

3. Some kids are like Sonya. They get mixed up about different *sounds* in words. But there are other children with language disorders like Eve's. They are good with the language sounds. But they have trouble understanding or using words and sentences correctly.

4. They can have a problem learning new vocabulary. They don't seem to know as many words as other kids. It may also be hard for them to learn about grammar and about the order of words in sentences.

5. Many children who have language disorders are very good at picturing things. They sometimes are able to make pictures of ideas in their minds instead of remembering

explanations from their teachers. If a teacher is describing a place, a child who likes to make mind pictures may make up an imaginary photograph of that place in his mind.

6. They may also have trouble with their attention. They stop listening because it is so hard for them to understand what people are saying. Eve did this sometimes.

Kids with language disorders can feel that they're not very smart. They don't realize that there are many different ways to be smart. Language is only one way. A kid with a language disorder might be very smart at fixing things, building things, enjoying music, solving math problems, helping people, or making friends. This child's kind of mind is just not working too well with language—at least not yet.

Help for Kids with Language Disorders

 Kids with language disorders may be able to get some help from a speech and language therapist. This is a person who helps kids improve in language. A speech and language therapist can give a kid exercises on the kinds of language mind work that are a problem.

Kids with language disorders should sit close to the teacher and practice listening extra carefully. They may need to ask the teacher to explain something again after class or after school. Sometimes a friend can explain what a teacher said.

They need a lot of practice with language. They need to be brave enough to keep talking at home, with friends, and in school. They should say as much as they can think of about their ideas or things that have happened. They should not just answer "yes" or "no" or "stuff" when someone asks them a question.

 Since kids with language disorders are often very good at picturing things, they can make charts or pictures on paper to understand things better. Sometimes a kid with a language disorder learns arithmetic best by studying finished problems. He decides it is easier to figure out how they were done than to understand a teacher's explanations.

They usually need extra help with certain skills, especially reading and writing. They may need a lot of help to improve their reading comprehension.

If kids with language problems don't talk enough in school or at home, their language problems may not improve fast enough.

Reading a lot can help language abilities, too. It is very important for kids with language disorders to read about things they like or know a lot about. Reading for fun can be fun! And it can help improve a kid's ability to do language kinds of mind work.

More about Social Skills Problems

Derek's kind of mind found it hard to make and keep friends. He kept annoying other kids, but he didn't realize it. He had a lot of trouble with his **social skills**.

A social skills problem is a learning disorder because kids like Derek have trouble learning how to get along with other people—just as Sonya had trouble learning to read.

Some Things to Know about Kids with Social Skills Problems

1. Kids are sometimes born with social skills problems! Kids like Derek have the kinds of minds that just don't know how to act so that other kids want to be with them. They do not know how to talk right with their classmates. They may try to brag. They may tell jokes that no one else thinks are funny. Often, they argue or they say things that make other kids feel angry.

2. They may do or say things that seem weird to other kids in school or around home. They don't *mean* to act weird. They just don't understand how they look or sound to everyone else.

3. They may seem too selfish. They may not be good at sharing. They may not know how to say or do things that will make other people feel good.

4. A lot of them try to act tough. That's what Derek did.

5. They are often picked on or bullied or made fun of by other kids. Sometimes popular kids can be mean. They do things to get everyone else to stay away from students with social skills problems.

6. Often, kids with social skills problems can't figure out why no one likes them. They would love to have friends and be popular. They just can't seem to understand why so many other kids don't like them.

7. They may spend a lot of time alone. Being alone so much can make them very sad.

When you have good social skills, you can have great times with other kids. Page 263 shows some important social skills.

Good Social Skills

Help for Kids with Social Skills Problems

Kids with social skills problems can improve their social skills. They can be taught how to act and what to say so others will like them better and want to be with them. There are social skills training groups for kids in many schools and towns. In these groups, kids get together and talk about their social lives with a grown-up who knows all about social skills.

They can get help from a parent. A parent can take a child out to lunch with another kid. That mother or father can listen and watch carefully while the two children are together. Later on, the parent can talk to the kid about what happened that day during lunch. A mother might say, "I noticed you were bragging all the time. You never said anything nice to Ricky during lunch. If you really want him to like you, you have to concentrate on saying some good things about him. You can't just brag about yourself." That kind of advice can be very helpful.

They should probably start working on making one or two good friends. Not everyone needs to be super popular.

Some kids don't have many friends because they just like doing things that are very different from what other kids like. There is nothing wrong with being different. You shouldn't change your interests or your ideas or the way you look just so other kids will like you. You need to be yourself. And you need to be proud of *your* kind of mind.

There are some students who enjoy being alone. They don't seem to need a lot of friends. Still, it sure feels excellent to have at least one or two close friends.

More about Motor Skills Problems

Your muscles work a lot like motors. So, it's not surprising that the things your muscles can do well are called your **motor skills**.

The motor or engine in a car can't work all by itself. It needs a driver to make it work—to turn it on and off and make it go fast or slowly. Your muscles can't work by themselves, either. They need to be controlled. The "driver" of your muscles is your mind. The control of your muscles is called **motor coordination**. So, motor coordination is a kind of mind work.

When you hop, or when you write your name without even thinking about it, you're using your motor coordination. Your mind is getting your muscles to do these skills automatically. Of course, when you're first learning to do something, your mind has to work hard to get your muscles to move just right.

Some children have trouble with their motor coordination. So it's really hard for them to learn motor skills. Some kids have trouble coordinating their big muscles—like the ones in their arms and legs. These kids have **gross motor problems**.

Other kids have trouble with their small muscles—like the ones in their fingers. These kids have **fine motor problems**. Derek had both gross and fine motor problems.

The diagram on page 268 shows examples of both fine motor skills and gross motor skills.

Motor Skills

	Gross Motor Skills (Using Your Large Muscles)	Fine Motor Skills (Using Your Small Muscles)
For Fun	Playing a Sport 	Tying a Knot
For Work (Which can also be fun!)	Shoveling Snow 	Writing a Report
Other Examples	Riding a Bicycle Climbing a Mountain Running in a Race Dancing Using a Skateboard	Fixing a Toy Cutting with Scissors Playing a Computer Game Sewing Building a Model

Some Things to Know about Fine Motor Problems

1. There are different kinds of fine motor problems. Many kids have a fine motor problem that makes it hard for them to write. But sometimes those kids can do other things with their fingers pretty well—like drawing or building models.

2. Kids who have a fine motor writing problem often hold a pencil in a way that's different from other kids. They may press too hard when they write. Then their hand may feel tired when they have to write a lot.

3. A lot of kids with fine motor problems can't write fast enough. They also have messy handwriting. Some of them have a lot of trouble learning how to do cursive handwriting. They say it's easier for them to print.

Sometimes students with fine motor writing problems are ashamed of their work. They feel very embarrassed if other kids see it. They may start to hate anything in school that has writing in it. So they write as little as possible. Then they don't get much practice. This makes it very hard for their writing to improve and get to be easier mind work.

Help for Kids with Fine Motor Problems

Students who have a hard time writing because of fine motor problems need to try out different kinds of pens and pencils. This way they can find something that feels good to write with. Some kids say it's hard for them to write with a ballpoint pen because it's too "slippery."

While they're trying to improve their writing, these kids can ask their teachers to give them more time to take tests or write reports. Or maybe they can be allowed to write a little less.

 Students with writing problems should practice by writing stories, keeping a diary, or writing about their hobbies and other things they are very interested in. The more these kids practice writing, the better they will get. It's important not to give up.

Kids with fine motor problems can get good at using a computer. Even if it isn't easy for them to use a keyboard, they should work at it. Someday they will probably be doing a lot of their schoolwork on a computer, and it will look really nice!

Everyone should have some fine motor success. So it's a good idea to find something you can do well with your hands—like fixing broken objects, doing a craft, or playing a musical instrument.

Some Things to Know about Gross Motor Problems

1. Kids with gross motor problems may look clumsy when they try to run, hop, or skip. This is because it's hard for their minds to control their large muscles well.

2. It can be very hard for kids with poor gross motor coordination to play sports well. They may have trouble throwing or catching or kicking a ball. They may get all mixed up and make too many mistakes during a game. Their minds have to work so hard to get

their muscles to work right that they sometimes forget what they're doing!

3. Often a kid with gross motor problems is a little afraid to do things with other kids. He may be afraid that the other kids will start playing some game or sport that he can't do well. So he may just stay at home and spend time by himself.

It is very cruel to laugh at a kid or to yell at him because he has trouble playing a sport. Children with gross motor problems already feel bad about themselves. We shouldn't make them feel worse.

Help for Kids with Gross Motor Problems

Kids with gross motor problems should try to find *one* sport to get really good at. This should be a sport that looks like fun and doesn't seem too hard.

They should try to find a grown-up who can practice with them and help them without a lot of other kids around.

They may need to talk with a coach or physical education teacher in school. This person can help kids improve. He or she can also make sure kids with gross motor problems are not too embarrassed in front of the other kids.

Exercise is really important for everybody. You have to get exercise to keep healthy. So, even if you're not good at sports, you need to find ways to keep your muscles working and playing hard. You don't need excellent motor coordination to hike or jog or do exercises.

All Kinds of Lives

There are all kinds of jobs to be done in our world. So, it's a good thing that we have all kinds of minds to do them. Luckily, every kind of mind has some kinds of mind work that it can do to make the world a much better place. But first we all need to understand our own minds.

Wouldn't it be great if we could all feel good about our own minds? Wouldn't it be fun if we could all enjoy and respect each others' kinds of minds? Then, we might live in a world where all kinds of minds would be happy and proud to be living all kinds of lives!

About Dr. Mel Levine
and His Kind of Mind

Dr. Mel Levine is a pediatrician, a doctor who just takes care of kids. He works mostly with children who are having some trouble learning or getting along in school. Many of them are just like the children in *All Kinds of Minds.*

Dr. Levine and all the people who work with him are trying to learn more about children with learning disorders. He travels all over the world helping other doctors and teachers understand how students learn best. He tries to help people make sure that all kinds of minds do well in school. He believes that no child should feel like a failure.

When he was young, Dr. Levine had some problems himself. In fifth grade, he didn't do much school work because mostly he wanted to play with his pets. And he was never very good at sports. Kids were very happy when he was on the other team! But he did have good social skills and a few good friends. He got along especially well with his collie whose name was Lady.

After fifth grade, Dr. Levine started to work very hard, and he did better and better in school. He became an excellent student in just about all subjects, except—of course—PE where he often got into trouble for forgetting his gym suit. Some people thought maybe he forgot it on purpose.

When he went to college at Brown University, Dr. Levine became a top student in his class. He won a special prize called a Rhodes Scholarship so he could study at Oxford University in England.

Dr. Levine was very young when he decided he wanted to be a doctor. After he returned from England, he went to Harvard Medical School where he learned how to be a children's doctor. Then he went to Asia where he took care of kids whose parents were in the Air Force. When he returned to the United States, he worked for a long time at the Children's Hospital in Boston. During this time he became more and more interested in taking care of children with school problems.

Dr. Levine and his wife now live in North Carolina on a farm called Sanctuary Farm. More than 150 geese from all over the world also live there. Dr. Levine thinks geese are great. Some people think it's funny (even a little weird) that he likes geese, but he just can't help it. His kind of mind finds geese quite interesting. He never gets bored when he is with them!

Some of Dr. Levine's geese have great social skills and are good at making lots of bird friends. Some others just like to show off and act cool all the time. Most of the geese are good at memory mind work. They never seem to forget anything. Many of them have awesome language skills, except that they use loud honks instead of words. A few of them have some trouble using the right kind of honk at the right time.

A lot of the geese are great at sports, especially in the water or in the air. But they can't climb trees, catch a ball, or ride a skateboard. Many of them are very, very alert, but a few of Dr. Levine's geese seem to have attention deficits. The ones with attention deficits are some of his best bird friends, even though they take mind trips!

On Sanctuary Farm, there are also nearly 40 pheasants, 7 swans, 2 herons, 4 large dogs, about 10 Maine Coon cats, 6 spotted Appaloosa horses, and a mule named Rose. Rose's kind of mind has excellent nose motor skills which she uses to open the latch on the barn door and tear open all the bags of goose food in the barn. Even though she tries to eat up all the food *and* the bags, she still makes a huge mess. Dr. Levine thinks that Rose the Mule might have some kind of feeding disorder.

Dr. Levine still doesn't play sports. He gets plenty of exercise, though, by carrying around heavy bags of goose food. And he builds up his muscles by cleaning up the barn after Rose tears up the feed bags and spreads goose food everywhere!

Thanks

I would like to thank all the people who helped me with the mind work for *All Kinds of Minds.*

I am especially grateful to Mary May who worked tenaciously for so many months—and with such impressive skill—to edit and polish these pages. I would also like to thank Jim Montgomery, Martha Reed, and Carl Swartz for reading (and tolerating) the manuscript during its earliest stages of development. In addition, I am extremely grateful for the ongoing support of my work from the following sources: The Geraldine R. Dodge Foundation, the Smart Family Foundation, The Robert Wood Johnson Foundation, The Federal Department of Education (Office of Special Education), the Bureau of Maternal and Child Health, and the Administration on Developmental Disabilities.

I also want to thank my parents who always respected my kind of mind, even though it was different from their kinds of minds! I also need to thank all the wonderful animals on my farm who have taught me that you don't have to be human to have an extraordinary kind of mind.

Finally, I thank my wife Bambi, who has influenced me in so many ways that are vividly reflected in these pages.

Mel Levine